READING THE DOG'S MIND

Training by Understanding

D1387222

John and Mary Holmes

RINGPRESS

Published by Ringpress Books Ltd,
PO Box 8, Lydney,
Gloucestershire GL15 6YD
Designed by Rob Benson

Discounts available for bulk orders
Contact the Special Sales Manager at
the above address. Telephone 01594 564222

First Published 1998
© 1998 RINGPRESS BOOKS

ISBN 1 86054 064 3

Printed and bound in Singapore

10 9 8 7 6 5 4 3 2

This book is for all the dogs who have shared our lives over the years.

To us, a life without dogs would be unthinkable. We have tried to understand them, but they have understood us much better; we have made mistakes, but they still did their best. They have taught us more than we taught them, and, over the years, we have learned to understand them better.

We hope this book will help readers to achieve a closer and more understanding relationship with their dogs.

CONTENTS

ACKNOWLEDGMENTS

NEIL EWART

Neil is the Breeding Manager for the Guide Dogs for the Blind Association. He is responsible for the production of all Guide Dog puppies in the UK; around 1,000 are bred each year at the Breeding Centre. He spent ten years as a Guide Dog Trainer and eight years as Training Manager at one of the organisation's centres.

HELEN McCAIN

Helen was a Guide Dog trainer who was seconded to the organisation Dogs for the Disabled when it was founded. She is now Head Trainer.

TENANT BROWNLEE

Tenant Brownlee has, sadly, died since writing his contribution. He was a well-known and respected gun dog trainer, and a regular contributor to the Kennel Gazette and other magazines.

CLAIRE GUEST

Claire is Training Manager for the organisation Hearing Dogs for Deaf People. Her hobby is training her own Springer Spaniels, with whom she has had considerable success in Field Trials.

PETER STOREY

Ex-Police Sergeant; Senior Home Office Accredited Instructor.

NEVILLE SHARP, BEM

Retired Police Sergeant; Home Office Qualified Police Dog Training Instructor; Team Leader, Calder Valley Search and Rescue Team.

COVER PHOTOGRAPHY: SALLY ANNE THOMPSON

Our thanks to all photographers who have contributed their work, and to Viv Rainsbury for her excellent line drawings.

INTRODUCTION

"The man who has conferred the greatest benefit upon the human race is the primitive savage who first tamed a litter of wolf cubs."

Sir Robert Ball LLD FRS.

It is often said, and with some truth, that you never really know a person until you live with them. Even then, it is doubtful that you will always understand their thoughts, their actions and the workings of their mind. Here, we are talking about our own species, *Homo sapiens*, so how much more difficult it is for us to understand another species, and for that species to understand us? *Canis Familiaris* – the domestic dog – has shared our homes and our lives for thousands of years, but is still often misunderstood.

ORIGINS

Recent DNA tests have proved that all dogs are descended from the wolf, and that domestication began about 135,000 years ago. It is only in the latter half of this century that scientists and behaviourists have started to investigate what makes a dog tick, and that dog owners are learning more about the dog's behaviour, instincts and senses. This does not mean that primitive man had no understanding of the wolves he took from the wild into the 'human pack' – in many ways, he would have been closer to this wild animal than the urbanised man of the 20th century is to his dog. Primitive man would have been much closer to nature, and he and the wolf would have had many similarities. He had

All breeds of dog are descended from the wolf.

a limited vocabulary, and no doubt relied on body language, as would the wolf. Both man and wolf are pack animals. In both packs, there would be a definite hierarchy, and the rules of the pack had to be obeyed. In the human pack, some men would be the hunters, and some would guard against enemies; the women would look after the children, gather and prepare food.

The youngsters, whether human or wolf, would, as they grew, join in the hunting expeditions, but take little part in the actual strategy of the chase until they were old enough and experienced enough to be useful members of the hunt. Small children would, unknowingly, have been practising the skills they would need as adults. They would have wrestled to test each other's strength, run races to improve their speed, played hide and seek and developed tracking skills. Wolf cubs would have played many similar games – wrestling with their litter mates, play-biting and chasing, squabbling over the food brought to them by the adults, and, before long, catching – or trying to catch – small prey such as insects and mice. In both cases, the youngsters learned

The domestic dog emerged through selective breeding, and there are some breeds that still bear a striking resemblance to the wolf.

Photo: Sheila Atter

discipline from the adults. No doubt most adults would put up with babies' and cubs' trying ways; but, as they grew older, a warning from a human adult, if not accepted, would no doubt have been followed by a clout around the earhole, or worse. The wolf cubs would have been warned by a soft growl, then a harsher one, which, if still ignored, would lead to a sudden, meaningful snap.

DOMESTICATION

Humans and wolves have proved through the ages that they are both survivors and opportunists, so it is not really surprising that, over the centuries, we have formed a relationship which has survived through innumerable changes in the world until the present day. It is without doubt the closest relationship we have with any of our domestic animals.

Science and technology may be able to give us the dates of certain events and to give the age of ancient skeletons. However, like much prehistory, we can only guess at why man decided to take the wolf into his life – or why the wolf decided to live with man. Both wolf and man competed for the same prey, and if food became scarce, then both must have needed to move on to fresh hunting grounds. At that time, man was a hunter/gatherer, and hungry wolves may well have scavenged around the camp sites for any human excreta, bones or leftover bits of food. Some might have been captured, killed and eaten, and their skins used for clothing. Some cubs, maybe orphan ones, could have been caught by the children and reared as pets or for food. Those that escaped the latter fate and joined the human pack would soon have proved useful on hunting expeditions, and as an early warning system when hostile tribesmen were approaching. As we said, however, we are only guessing.

The earliest evidence of the domesticated dog is from a grave in Germany from about 14,000 BC. By that time, man had progressed from stone axes to arrows tipped with small stone blades. This obviously improved his hunting ability, and the tamed wolf would have been a great asset in tracking, killing or holding at bay wounded game.

The concepts of genetics were unheard of in those times, but man must soon have realised that 'like begets like', and, very gradually over the centuries, would have bred for specific qualities – speed for hunting, scenting ability for tracking, keen hearing for guarding, and so on. At that time, there were many different species of wolf all over the world. These varied in size, colour and length of coat. As man became more peripatetic, these different types would have interbred. This interbreeding, coupled with man's selection for the type he wanted, resulted in the gradual emergence of the domestic dog. The Russian fox fur farmer, Belyaev, wrote in 1979 of his experiment to selectively breed Silver Foxes for a placid temperament, which meant they would be much easier to handle in their cages on the fox farms. He found that they changed physically as well as mentally. He experimented over 20 years, choosing his stock from over 10,000 foxes on various farms. Not only did the foxes become friendly, they wagged their tails, developed drop ears, black and white coats and curly tails.

DOGS THROUGH THE AGES

Not until the fifth millennium BC is there evidence that prehistoric dogs were starting to develop into distinctive breeds. When the Europeans arrived in Australia in the 19th century, the Aborigines appeared to have a relationship with the Dingo which was probably very similar to that which early man had with the first domesticated wolves. Some Dingoes were kept as pets, others were fattened up and eaten, and some were kept as hunting dogs. The Australian writer, Meggitt, quoting Lumholzt, who wrote about Aborigines and dingoes in 1889, says "Its master never strikes but merely threatens. He caresses it like a child, eats the fleas off it, then kisses its snout." However, it was also said that these tamed Dingoes were usually very poorly fed and left to scavenge for themselves.

Compared with the dogs of long ago, most 20th century dogs have a cushy time of it today, but are they happier? Although the way many dogs were treated appears very cruel to us, many led interesting and active lives. Some, such as the Pekingese of the Chinese Emperors, were better treated than the Palace slaves, and it is said that they were often suckled by women slaves whose unwanted baby girls had been killed! The Romans had hunting dogs and war dogs, but also kept pet dogs. They exported hundreds of English Mastiffs to Rome, either to fight in the arena or to be trained as war dogs. Some of the war dogs would wear suits of armour, with soft cloth underneath to prevent chafing from the metal chain. They would also have had collars with knives attached to inflict damage on the enemy and their horses. Small pet dogs were also quite common and the poet Martial (c.40 – c.102AD)

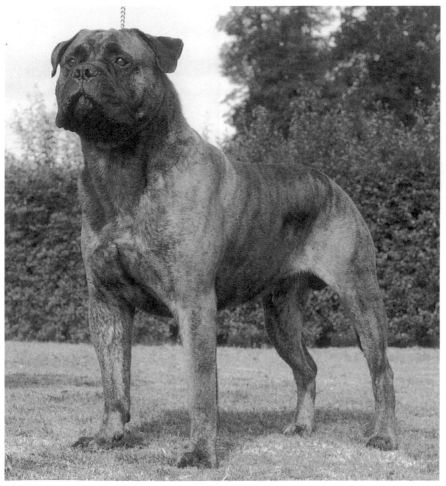

Dogs of the Mastiff type were the traditional dogs of war.

The St Bernard: A noble dog of great sagacity, famous as the first mountain rescue dog.

said of his friend's dog: "Issa is purer than the kiss of a dove, she is more tender than all the young maidens and more precious than sapphire." Pliny the Elder (23 – 79AD) was also impressed with dogs, recording that they were the most faithful, bar none, of all animals.

In Homer's *Odyssey* there is a story that any trainer of today's police dogs will appreciate. Odysseus disguised himself as a beggar and was approaching the outskirts of his territory for the purpose of calling on his swineherd, Eumaeus, when noisy dogs barking loudly suddenly attacked. If he had not had the presence of mind to sit down and drop his staff he would probably have had a bad time. "Old man", said the

The Cavalier King Charles Spaniel: A royal favourite.

Photo: Carol Ann Johnson.

swineherd, "that was a narrow escape. The dogs would have made short work of you and the blame would have fallen on me." Cicero wrote that "Dogs watch for us faithfully; they love and worship their masters; they hate strangers; their power of tracking by scent is extraordinary; great is their keenness to chase – what can all this mean but that they were made for man's advantage?"

When Henry VIII of England made an alliance with Charles V of Spain, he sent a draft of soldiers and a battalion of 800 dogs to fight for him. In the reign of Queen Elizabeth I, a battalion of 600 dogs belonging to the Earl of Essex was sent to help quell the disorders in Ireland.

Sled dogs were invaluable to the survival of the Eskimos of the frozen North, and, later on, to the early explorers. Although used for work, it is interesting to note that Captain Scott (of the Antarctic) wrote in his diary a very pertinent remark about his Huskies: "A dog must be either eating, asleep or interested – the dog is almost human in his demand for living interest."

The Collie: Bred to herd stock.   *Photo: Keith Allison.*

In 1728, Oliver Goldsmith wrote of the dogs of the Grande St. Bernard Hospice: "They have a breed of noble dogs whose extraordinary sagacity often enables them to rescue the traveller, though the perishing men may be 10 or 20 feet below the snow. The delicacy of smell which they can trace him offers a chance of escape."

Of the older breeds, Pekes, Pugs, Maltese Terriers and (no doubt) others would have been kept as pets, mainly by the Lords and Ladies of the Court, and, of course, by Kings, such as Charles and his Cavalier Spaniels. Pepys wrote in his diary: "All I observed was the silliness of the King, playing with his dogs all the while and not minding his business."

For centuries, hounds have been used for hunting, Mastiff types as guard dogs and for fighting alongside soldiers. Collies herded stock, and the European sheepdogs guarded the flocks from predators. Dogs have mainly done the task for which they were bred, and there is no better reward for a dog than doing just that.

Most dogs are adoptable and are able to fit into modern society.

THE MODERN DOG

In the latter half of this century, man has been to the moon, computers are commonplace, every home has electrical gadgets, radios and televisions. The majority of homes have central heating and nearly all families have cars. Dogs are adaptable creatures, thankfully; they have to be to live in the modern world. Central heating causes flea infestations, which are then treated with a bewildering array of chemicals. The dog no longer has a juicy bone to chew on, but is usually fed a complete, dry dog food. He has to become used to staying alone in the house as his owners go out to work, although his genes still tell him he is a pack animal. Many dogs spend a considerable amount of time in cars. Fewer and fewer are allowed the opportunity to run free, something we consider that every dog should be allowed to do. Because of local laws and various 'dog-free' zones, it can be difficult to find anywhere to take them. All of this makes it even more important for owners to understand their dogs. Even if we cannot offer them an ideal life, we can, and should, make every effort to understand their needs, and, in return for the companionship and loyalty they offer us, give them as happy a lifestyle as we possibly can.

CHAPTER ONE

THE DOG'S WORLD

The dog's world is, in many ways, similar to our own, but it is very different in other ways. Although we share most of the same instincts and senses, our own have become blunted by so-called civilisation. Dogs react to their instincts and senses far more spontaneously and in greater depth than we do. To understand your dog, you must realise how much his behaviour is governed by his instincts.

SIGHT

Until quite recently, it had always been thought that dogs were only capable of seeing in black and white, but scientists have now decided that they can see both blue and green and can also recognise combinations of these colours. Like us, some dogs have better eyesight than others, but it varies from breed to breed, and in some instances their sight is not as good as ours. Dogs' night sight is generally superior to ours, but they also tend to be short-sighted. Their ability to focus is limited, and most dogs have problems seeing a stationary object. However, their field of vision is far wider, usually about 200 degrees, or even more, whereas man's range is about 150 degrees. Breeds where the eyes are set at the side of the head have the widest range. Breeds with protruding eyes, or with very deep set eyes, often have less keen sight. Dogs are also able to detect the slightest movement, a necessity for any predator.

USING SIGHT

We have worked with dogs for many years, and over that time we have had many examples of how dogs use – or do not use – their sight. During the last war, Mary was in the Army and had a small Collie called Honey. When at home on leave, she often left Honey with her mother, who would take the dog for walks. If Honey spotted anyone in khaki

Dogs are much better than us at detecting even the slightest movement.
Photo: Sally Anne Thompson.

on the opposite side of the road, she would dash over to them if not stopped. If there was someone in Air Force blue, she ignored them. The difference between the two colours is slight but was obvious to the dog.

Often, we will tell a dog to go and pick up a ball or other toy from a flat surface, such as a carpet or short grass. An excitable dog may well rush straight past, or even trip over it, appearing not to see it at all, but suddenly he will pick up the scent, grab the toy and bring it back. He is not being stupid, but doing what comes naturally – using his superior sense of smell rather than his eyesight.

Many owners teach their dogs to catch a ball or a Frisbee, and find some dogs much better at it than others. In some dogs, the position of the eye makes it difficult for the dog to focus on the thrown object, but, given time and patience, most dogs will learn to catch successfully in the end, especially if the catch is something like a bit of dried liver!

When we go out to check our sheep, John often goes one way round and Mary the other. Mary usually has our dog, Tolly, with her. When Mary sees John in the distance, she sends Tolly to him. Tolly will race off in the direction indicated, and, if John is stationary, will give no sign of having seen him but will suddenly pick up his scent on the wind and rush up to him. If he is moving she will see him immediately and go straight to him.

Blind dogs often seem to manage to find their way about remarkably well and to lead happy lives. John once saw a quite amazing example of a blind Border Collie working sheep. The dog belonged to the late, famous Sheepdog Trial man, Willie Wallace. The dog had been a well-known Trial winner and did not go blind until much later in life. As a Trial dog, he had been trained to answer to whistle and verbal commands. Willie sent him out round the sheep, where he performed a classical 'outrun and fetch'. He was controlled by verbal and whistle commands to move right or left, come on and stop. The dog had complete control over the sheep and it was almost impossible to believe that he was totally blind. John believes he could hear and smell the sheep, but his control was uncanny.

Because dogs are so good at detecting even the slightest movement,

*Retrieving
provides both
exercise and fun.*

some owners cannot understand how their dog knows when they are
going shopping, for a walk or even away on holiday. To the dog it is
simple. Someone pulls the car keys out of their pocket, changes their
shoes, picks up a wallet. All little things, but ones that tell the dog what

is going to happen. Not so long ago, 'talking and counting' dogs were quite common in circuses or in Music Hall acts. These dogs would appear to be able to count, add and subtract, answer questions and say whether something was right or wrong. All by barks, one for yes and two for no, and the right number for the arithmetic. As far as could be seen, the handler just asked the dog questions, but in reality he was giving some very small sign. It could be as small as blinking an eye, scratching his nose, taking his hand out of his pocket, touching an ear, or any other inconspicuous movement the dog was trained to watch for.

SMELL

Of all the dog's senses, the sense of smell is by far the most important. A dog with no sense of smell is rather like a blind person. It could well

The dog's amazing sense of smell has been put to many uses. Here, a Springer Spaniel is searching for smuggled drugs.
                    Photo courtesy: Metropolitan Police.

be said that the dog lives in a world of scent – his sense of smell is at least a million times greater than ours.

Man has put the dog's amazing scenting abilities to many uses. They are trained to detect drugs (even when hidden in places such as petrol tanks), to find lost people, to detect explosives, to track criminals and to find people buried under an avalanche, to name but a few. Compared with a dog's sense of smell, our own is quite weak and no-one, not even the scientist, really understands how the dog can detect minute quantities of drugs or follow a trail many days old.

The structure of the dog's nose is very complicated and quite different from the human nose. To make full use of his nose, the dog must keep it clean. A dirty nose, irritated by dust or other forms of contamination, would be far from effective. Having no handkerchief, the dog cleans his nose by licking it.

In the same way that high-pitched noises can upset a dog's sensitive hearing, so very strong smells can be off-putting for many dogs. House-proud dog owners who are constantly spraying rooms with highly perfumed air-fresheners are doing their dogs no favours.

Newborn pups appear to have some sense of smell, but it is nothing like as acute as that of older dogs. At a very early age, the puppy relies more on touch, but in a matter of weeks, the pups in a litter can be seen sniffing the air to detect strange smells, sniffing any strange objects or using their noses to check up on each other. When first offered solid food, pups will usually nose it and sniff it before tasting it. Once familiar with the smell, this preliminary investigation is quickly dropped and the food gulped down. Pups will investigate any toys or strangers by smelling them. They do this because their brains are geared to translate all these different smells. A puppy's nose will tell him far more about his environment than his eyes and ears will.

All dogs have sacs on either side of the anus containing a fluid with a pungent smell. To us, they all smell the same (and it is a pretty nasty smell, too), but, to a dog, each one is different. Each dog has his own individual smell, which gives him his own 'identity card' as far as other canines are concerned.

The wolf uses this superior sense of smell in many aspects of his life. It enables him to recognise individual members of his own pack, to discover if strange wolves have been in his territory and how long it has been since they left. He knows when a female is ready for breeding and he can tell where another wolf has been and what he has just eaten – all this information, and much more, from his acute sense of smell. He can also use it to track down his prey, find a water source and to give him warning of any dangers such as his arch enemy – man.

SOCIAL SNIFFING

Once we realise what a significant part scent plays in a dog's life, we must use some common sense in dealing with occasional problems this causes. For instance, we may not like it much when our dog trots up to another one in the park and they start sniffing each other's rear ends, but they are only doing what comes naturally. To call him away and tell him not to be 'dirty' is useless and unkind. What he is doing is normal canine greeting behaviour. Owners who interfere are more likely to cause trouble than if the dogs are left to themselves. Most dogs sort things out peacefully. Those which do not are usually the ones which have been deprived of social contact with other puppies and dogs when young. There can be, and often is, a problem with dogs who have not learned proper canine behaviour as puppies. Luckily, this problem can be solved by taking your puppy to a good puppy socialisation class. It is important to emphasise the word 'good'. A number of well-meaning people start up these classes without really understanding what they are doing. If a tiny Yorkshire Terrier pup is flattened by a thumping but well-meaning Labrador pup, the class is unlikely to be of much help. A good class, run by an experienced and understanding trainer, can help to give the pup a really good start in life. Classes should not only have puppies; there should be a few older dogs with the right sort of temperament to teach them how to behave with their superiors. A young pup will usually approach in a submissive manner, roll over to expose his tummy, which the older dog will sniff until he decides the pup is behaving properly and can now play.

Two dogs meet for the first time.

The first approach is sniffing nose to nose.

Next, the groin is sniffed.

Play is initiated.

Play starts.

There are, obviously, some occasions when you have to draw the line. If you have a smartly-dressed lady visitor and your friendly Irish Wolfhound shoves his big, cold nose up her skirt to find out a bit more about her, you cannot expect her to be pleased. As an alternative to shoving his nose up skirts, teach your dog to sit and 'shake hands' – a more civilised form of greeting, and one which the dog will happily accept as, to him, it is a natural action. If you do not teach him an alternative but shout at him for his friendly, nose-nudging greeting, you will simply end up with a very confused dog.

When you have been away and your dog greets you, he will almost certainly give you a good sniffing, and, so long as you allow this around your feet and hands, he should be satisfied. He will have discovered if you have been to visit a friend – human or canine, been on the train or maybe to the hairdresser's. He cannot ask you where you were, but his nose can help him to find out.

NEW SURROUNDINGS

A walk in the country, beside the sea, or in any fresh area will provide your dog with endless delight. Just as you look around to find out what is worth seeing, your dog will sniff around to find out what goes on in this place. He will smell the ground, trees, grass, footprints, any dropped litter, dog and other animal faeces and a whole lot more. He may find the scent of a rabbit or a squirrel which dashed up a tree, or a lost ball hidden in a bush. His discoveries are endless and will provide him with immense pleasure. He might even do some detective work. Once we were out riding in the woods and the Collie we had with us disappeared into the undergrowth. We called her out, but she kept returning. So we rode over to see what she had found, and it was a safe which had been broken into from a very well-known firm. We contacted the police, and the firm's chairman was so grateful that he sent along half-a-dozen bottles of whisky. We are not suggesting that you allow your dog to stop and sniff every time he wants to do so, or let him investigate one spot for half an hour, but just as you stop to look at the view every now and then, let him stop and sniff.

USING SCENT

Obviously, police dogs, guide dogs, dogs for the disabled and other working dogs must learn that they cannot go around sniffing indiscriminately all the time. Once trained to do a specific job, they learn to concentrate on that job while working. This is not to say that they should not have the chance to behave in a normal way when off duty. Even drug detection dogs are taken out in the fields to relax and run around freely.

It is because of this ability to detect different scents that the dog has been trained to help man in so many ways. The ones who qualify after training usually have a happy and rewarding life, doing a job they enjoy because they are using one of their keenest senses.

As far as the pet dog is concerned, he can, with a little effort on the part of his owners, be taught 'games' where he can use his nose and have fun at the same time. There are very few dogs who cannot be taught to retrieve – and many which never need teaching, particularly the gun dog breeds. Once a dog retrieves, you can make endless opportunities for him to use his nose. Children love playing hide and seek, and the dog can soon be taught to go and find them. Either in the house or when out for a walk, articles can be hidden and the dog sent to find them, or he can be taught to 'seek back', and find an article you have dropped whilst walking along. This can be very useful if you drop a wallet, a glove or something similar in a field. We once had a Cocker Spaniel, Flush. Apart from being a well-known film-star, she had a quite exceptional nose. If a blade of grass was knotted and thrown down, she would search around and find it. Once, when working in London, John lost his car keys in Hyde Park. Luckily, he had Flush with him and she quickly found them, quite a way back along where he had walked.

Small and large dogs can both have good scenting ability. We have a small Chihuahua who enjoys nothing better than searching for a fir cone thrown into heather, where there are heaps of other cones. She may take a long time but never gives up and always comes back with the right one.

If you are competitive and have a gun dog breed, there are always gun dog tests and trials. To deny a gun dog the right to use his nose is verging on cruelty.

ROLLING

While we are on the subject of scent, there is one thing on which neither the experts nor the scientists agree. It is the question of why dogs roll in (what, to us, are) disgusting substances such as dog faeces, cow dung, dead rabbits and the like. There are various theories, but no-one knows for sure. Some dogs never do this, and if you have one of these, you are lucky. Others seem to take every opportunity they can. If you watch carefully, you can often stop a dog from rolling before he really gets down to it. There are tell-tale signs such as prolonged sniffing, a lowering of the head and a sideways turn. If you manage to shout "No" just before he goes down you might stop him. If not, then there is nothing for it but a bath. Strange as it may seem, the best thing for getting rid of the smell of fox or skunk is tomato ketchup – no, we have no idea why, but it really does work.

HEARING

The dog's sense of hearing is much greater than our own. A person with average hearing will recognise sounds of up to 20,000 cycles per second, but a dog with good hearing will hear sounds of up to 35,000 cycles, or possibly more. Dogs can also locate sounds very accurately, an

Dogs locate the source of sound much more accurately than humans.
Photo: Sally Anne Thompson.

ability which could be helped by the fact that they can move their ears independently – a skill which few humans can manage! For the dog, it does help to fix the direction of the sound. They can also hear very slight sounds, such as a rabbit hopping through the grass some way off, or the tiny squeak of a mouse.

Because the dog can hear high-frequency sounds, what some people call a 'silent whistle' is often used in training, which humans hear only faintly or not at all. This can work very well with some dogs, but others with sensitive hearing can quickly become upset by it. If you want to use one, borrow one first to make sure that it does not upset your dog.

A dog lying asleep on the hearth will often jump up, wag his tail and rush to the door. Several minutes later, his master will drive up in the car, home from work, but no-one else will have heard the sound. If your dog growls or barks when all seems quiet, he is probably hearing an intruder in the garden, someone approaching the door or possibly even breaking into the garden shed. So do not be in too much of a hurry to tell him to shut up because you cannot hear anything – one of the reasons dogs are used as guards in the armed forces is their acute hearing.

LOUD NOISES

When talking to your dog, training him or just playing with him, do not shout. He can hear you perfectly well – he may not want to hear you, but he can, and shouting will not help. In fact, nothing will make a dog disobedient more quickly than someone who keeps shouting his name or calling him when he takes no notice. His name, or whatever you are shouting at him, becomes, as far as he is concerned, just another noise which he gets used to and ignores. It has been recognised for some time that people living near airports, working in noisy factories or even dancing in discos can suffer physical and mental damage from the excess noise. Try to imagine what excess noise does to your dog. Sound waves cause pressure on eardrums, and, if the noise is really intolerable, then it can cause pain and distress as well as damaging the eardrums.

A considerable number of dogs are afraid of thunder. It is often thought that they react to the change in atmospheric pressure before a thunderstorm, but we recently heard a veterinary surgeon saying that he had a bitch who hated thunderstorms, but who went deaf in her old age. She then completely ignored the storms that had previously made her go berserk. His opinion was that the dog had such acute hearing that she heard the thunder long before the people in the house did.

VOCALISATION

Although we have a language, of which we make good use, the dog also has quite a repertoire of vocal sounds – some soft, some loud and all with different meanings. A bark is the sound most commonly associated with the dog, but not only are there varieties of barks, there are many other sounds which the dog uses to communicate with other dogs, with humans and, to a certain extent, with other animals.

DOG COMMUNICATION

Puppies start to learn to communicate when in the nest, and vocalising is one of the ways that they do this. A newborn usually takes a breath and then lets out a cry as his mother starts to clean him up. He soon learns that, if he rolls away from his mother and his siblings and cannot find his way back, if he squeaks and whimpers, the odds are that mother will reach out and haul him back to the milk bar. Some bitches 'talk' to their pups, making a soft, crooning, grunting sound. In a litter of wild dogs, when the pups are a little older, a sharp warning bark from mother makes them scuttle back to their nest or, if too far away, they will 'freeze' until the danger is past. As they grow, the pups start to yap when they play and, if one bites too hard, the other one squeals and generally bites him back, so the game has to stop.

HOWLING

No-one has ever come up with a complete answer as to why dogs howl. It is thought that, when wolves decide to go hunting, they often start

In hunt kennels, the hounds will howl or sing, possibly a throwback to wolf behaviour.

howling as a means of getting the pack together. Packs of hounds howl or 'sing' in their kennels. A lonely wolf may howl in an effort to make contact with others.

We had a Basset Hound called Bertie who, to put it kindly, did not have a very high IQ! Given the slightest opportunity, Bertie would go off hunting in the forest nearby. He always gave tongue when on a scent, and, as he never went very far, we

At the start of a hunt, wolves will howl to get the pack together.

would sometimes follow the sound, catch him and bring him home. At other times, he would get completely lost. In that case, he would sit down wherever he was and lift up his head and howl and howl until someone found him and brought him home! In his case, it was a very effective means of communication.

COMMUNICATING WITH OTHER ANIMALS

Not only do dogs make a very good job of understanding us, but, when mixing with other animals, they soon learn which sounds are friendly, menacing or frightened. Our cats have had no trouble learning dog language, and a new cat who is not sure of the dogs will have no problem giving a loud hiss which tells the dogs exactly what he thinks.

Cattle being fetched in by a dog quickly learn that his bark means "get a move on!"; and sheep on a hill hiding in thick bracken will start to move when they hear a Sheepdog's bark getting closer.

COMMUNICATING WITH PEOPLE

Owners learn, or should learn, to understand the different barks which their dog gives. There is a warning bark to tell of approaching strangers, a welcoming bark for friends, and, often, a special bark for members of the family. There is an excited play-bark and, when having a game, a dog will also produce a non-threatening play-growl, which sounds nothing like the growl used as a warning to keep off.

When being petted, dogs often heave great sighs or give soft grunts. Submissive dogs will whine or whimper when confronted by a more dominant dog. Many submissive or nervous dogs often whimper when seeking attention from their owners.

Dogs are much quicker at picking up our language than we are at understanding theirs, but once a dog has been living with you for a while, it is not too difficult to recognise his different barks and growls. Most dogs, once house-trained, realise that, if they bark at the door, they will be let out. Some, with rather more stupid owners, bark in vain, pee on the door mat and get into trouble, so always make an effort to see what it is your dog wants to tell you.

No-one wants a noisy dog, but to stop a dog from barking and letting off steam is verging on cruelty. It would be like telling children let out of school that they must be quiet! This is not to say your dog can bark every time he feels like it; only when you say so. The best time is when he is taken for a walk in the country and can run free. The best way to teach a dog to stop barking is to teach him to bark on command and then to teach him to stop.

As we said previously, there is no need to shout at a dog, as he hears much better than you do. Talk to him softly, and if you are telling him to do something, do so firmly – not loudly. It does not matter what you say to him; what matters is your tone of voice. You can call him a bad dog in a joky, friendly tone and he will wag his tail. Tell him he is a bad dog and growl it out at him and he will know that this time you mean it. When you praise him, put some enthusiasm into it. If you say "That was very clever" in a completely flat tone, it means nothing to the dog. The more you understand how to communicate with your dog, the happier you will both be.

TASTE

Not a great deal is known about the dog's sense of taste, except that the dog has many fewer taste buds than we do, and so, compared with us, has a poor sense of taste. It has been shown that dogs have more taste buds which respond to sugars than to other tastes. Many of us know that our dog has what is termed a 'sweet tooth', which is not to say that sugary items are good for him. In the wild, wolves and wild dogs seek out and enjoy such things as wild blackberries, strawberries and raspberries, all of which contain fruit sugars, which in turn supply energy.

When we first moved to our present farm, we had a large number of dogs which we used to exercise on a disused railway line. The banks were covered in sweet, wild strawberries in early summer. Unfortunately, we seldom managed to have any, as the dogs usually cleared the lot! The larger dogs would also pick off the ripe blackberries, to the annoyance of the smaller ones, who could not reach that high.

Although classed as carnivores, most dogs are omnivores. The dog is an opportunist and can, and often does, eat literally anything he can find. Although the dog has an inferior sense of taste to us, he has a superior sense of smell. A dog will smell the potential food item before he tastes it, and, often, the smellier it is, the better. A long-dead rabbit on a country walk or the contents of a dustbin – both are acceptable.

FEEDING

Dogs do not have what we would term 'good table manners'. In the wild, when the pack makes a kill, it is no use hanging about hoping that someone will leave you a share. A wild dog never knows when he will get his next meal or what it will be. He may come across a dead deer, which will provide him with a meal without his having to expend any energy on hunting. If he is part of a pack, there could be a successful hunt ending in the kill of some large prey, which would provide food for several days. At other times, game might be scarce, and he would have to make do with mice and voles, or no food at all. The dog's stomach can hold a vast amount, and, if he has a huge meal one day, he is quite content to go without the next.

Today, we are all advised to feed our dogs every day at the same time

and on the same food, which is certainly not natural for the dog, and can store up trouble for the owner. If a dog is always fed at exactly the same time every day and on the same food, what happens if the owner runs out of food or cannot get home to feed the dog at 6pm? The owner gets worried, the dog becomes

Pups need regular feeding, but for adults it is better to vary mealtimes.

worked up, paces about, whines and becomes generally upset because he does not understand why his dinner is not there. There are bound to be times when he cannot have his dinner on time, so, as long as he gets his dinner, feed him when it suits you. If he is not expecting it at 4pm, he will be delighted to have it then or later, so long as he gets it. We had some friends who had a Flatcoat Retriever puppy and who went to endless lengths to feed him four times a day, at exactly 8am, noon, 4pm and 8pm. If they could not arrive home in time, they became extremely worried that it would upset the pup. The pup stayed with us for a couple of days, and very soon found that life was a bit more exciting if he did not know when or what he was having for dinner!

When we did film and television work with our dogs, they were never fed until they had finished working for the day. If it was very late, which it often was, then they would not be fed that day, but would have a larger meal the next day. It would have been impractical for us to interrupt a scene because the dog's dinner was due! Because our dogs were used to it, it never worried them. At one time, we had large boarding kennels, and we always fasted the dogs one day a week – we still do. The fussy ones ate up better, and the fat ones maybe got a little slimmer.

DIET

Everyone has their own idea of what is best for their dogs, so we are not going to go into details of all the different diets available today, except to say that we feed biscuit meal (kibble) and meat, with the addition of leftover table scraps, minced vegetables and, several times a week, we give our dogs a good, sturdy bone. Dogs have eaten bones for thousands of years, yet today, many are denied that pleasure. Bones help to keep teeth clean, which is nicer for the dog and cheaper than doggy toothpaste. A dog eating a bone exercises most of his muscles, especially those in his neck and jaw when he holds the bone down with his feet and pulls off the meat. A dog with his head stuck in a bowl of complete diet just gulps it down, and one of the most enjoyable events of his day is over in seconds.

Today, most trainers recommend using food treats as a reward when training. If you do this, do not forget that the dog will need a smaller meal when his dinner is due. Small pieces of cooked liver make good rewards and are not fattening. Do not let your dog get into the habit of begging at the table; if you cannot stop him, shut him out of the room, and, remember, only give rewards when they have been earned.

It is well known in the horse world that feeding can have a great effect on the performance of the individual horse. Similarly, a change of diet can help to calm down a hyperactive dog. The majority of so-called 'complete' dog foods have far too high a protein content. Recently, special diets for working dogs, racing dogs, obedience dogs, old dogs, young dogs, sled dogs, gun dogs and so on have appeared on the market. There are, of course, some medical conditions which cause a dog to put on weight but, in the majority of cases, if a dog is too fat, it is the owner's fault. Your pet dog should not need all these fancy (and usually expensive) diets. Old-fashioned meat and biscuit, scraps, processed raw vegetables and fruit, raw bones, wholemeal pasta – all make good food for dogs. If your dog is the active type and has a lot of exercise, he will need more food than an old, rather more sedate type.

Dogs enjoy bones which help to clean teeth and exercise jaw muscles.
Photo: Marc Henrie.

It really is just common sense; if your dog looks well and obviously feels well, then you have got his diet right.

TOUCH

Puppies and babies are very similar in some ways. Neither can talk or understand what is dangerous and what is not. Both can, and do, learn by experience and experiment, and touch play is a very important part of early learning.

Some modern trainers think that to reward a dog by fondling him is very inefficient, as touch is not important to them. This is something with which we disagree. Very young puppies, whose senses of smell, hearing and sight are either non-existent or very slight, use touch to keep in contact with their dam and siblings. Other trainers, and there are many of them, say that you should give your dog a hug every day to make him happy – and why not? Your children enjoy a hug, and the dog is part of the family, so he should have his share of hugs too.

A study of small children of between three and four years old and their interactions with dogs showed that 67% of that interaction involved body contact. Another study showed that touching was people's most frequent behaviour when with a dog. A photographic competition in 1985 (Katcher & Beck) found that over 90% of the people and animals were touching each other. Therapy dogs provide enormous pleasure and help to both children and adults, many ill or withdrawn. The dogs reach out to touch them with paws or push a cold nose into their hands, and both humans and dogs enjoy the attention and petting which usually follows.

IN THE LITTER
As soon as they are born, healthy puppies squirm and wriggle their way to the warmth of their dam's body and to the milk bar. As they grow, pups can often be found lying in a heap, one on top of another. When one stirs and decides he is hungry, he pushes his way out, and the others, feeling the movement, soon follow. Once at the milk bar, they

*Pups reach up to paw their mothers milk – a natural behaviour
which is often used when adult dogs want to attract attention.*
Photo: Sally Anne Thompson.

nudge and push with their noses and often reach up with one paw in a
sort of begging action – all of which encourages the dam to let her milk
down. As they grow, pups often feed from the bitch when she is
standing up; they sit back on their hunkers and paw at her with both
paws doing a balancing act. Again this stimulates the milk flow.

A nursing bitch will have a great deal of physical contact with her
litter. A straying pup will be scooped back with a paw or lifted by the
scruff and dumped back with his siblings. The bitch licks them, cleans
them up, and, when they are very young, cuddles them to her. As they
grow, she plays with them but also disciplines them and teaches them
correct behaviour, which is important for any pack animals. If a pup
becomes too boisterous or bites a teat too hard, or tries to get some
milk when there is none, the dam will growl at him and seize him by
the nose and push him to the ground, still growling. When she lets him
go, the rest of the pups have usually got the message and leave her alone
– but they are not scared of her. Very soon they will be back, one pup
waving a paw and licking his lips and squirming up to her. The pups

are quickly learning the right response to aggressive behaviour.

Not many breeders today allow their male dogs to interact with their pups, but those who do have found it very interesting. The dog is often a tougher teacher than the bitch. He is usually friendly and even tolerant of the pups, but, if they insist on annoying him, he growls and very quickly seizes one round the muzzle and has him on the ground, but he does not hurt the pup. He is just teaching him to respect the pack leader; they are not afraid of him, but are learning how to behave with him. Some male dogs appear to 'set up' their pups. We heard of one who used to take his bone into the nest to allow the pups to play with it. One day, he obviously thought that they were ready for their first lesson. By this time, they were older, and playing about outside. The dog walked up to them with a large bone in his mouth, and put it down near them. As they rushed at it, he growled and pounced, grabbing the first one by the muzzle, letting him go and continuing the warning until the pups realised that, this time, it was his bone, and they were not allowed to touch it. This is a lesson humans could do well to remember.

MANNERS

Dogs wanting attention – often the submissive ones – will nudge their owner's hand with their nose, or even push their nose right into the hand. Although this is a friendly, attention-seeking action, it can develop into a nuisance unless the dog is taught when he can do it and when he can not. For instance, we once had an old Collie bitch who delighted in going up to any visitor (although not us – she knew better) and pushing her nose up under a cup of tea held in their hands – not popular! Neither is it popular when a large Irish Wolfhound wants to make friends by shoving his nose up a lady's skirt. Luckily, most dogs can either teach themselves to 'shake hands' – the same action they used on their dams – or can easily be taught. This makes a good substitute for nose nudging. The dog is happy because he is not being ticked off for what, to him, was meant to be a friendly gesture, and the visitors will certainly be much happier.

The puppy nudges his mother for attention.

The adult dog uses the same behaviour to get attention from his owner.

It can be very unkind and frustrating for the dog if we try to stop all his friendly gestures, his pleasure of welcoming a member of the pack home. Other instances are when he jumps up to greet you as you arrive back from work. If you just shout at him, he will not know why. Teach him to sit and shake hands instead, and you will both be happy. Some dogs persist in licking your hands or your face, if they can manage it. Although some owners encourage 'kissing', others, including ourselves, are not over-enthusiastic about it. However, as far as the dog is concerned, he is only trying to express his affection, which means that you should not be angry with him for doing what he thinks is the right action. Instead, if he is licking your hand, simply take it away, or, if he is licking your face, turn it away from him, and at the same time say "No" firmly. If he was welcoming another dog in this manner and the other one had had enough, he would simply ignore him, and, in that way, there would be no hard feelings. Depending on how it is used, touch can be a help to calm a dog, encourage him, help him to make friends and so on. It has been proved that massaging helps a dog to keep fit mentally and physically. Some Animal Welfare Centres have staff trained in the technique of the Tellington Touch, and they find that it helps aggressive or disturbed rescued dogs to settle down more quickly.

Apart from verbal warnings, a dog needing correction can be dealt with in a similar manner to that used by his dam when he was a puppy. Either take him on either side of the scruff, stare him straight in the eye and shake him, or grab him round the muzzle and push him down for a few seconds.

Dogs, like us, vary in nature, and some are more sensitive to touch than others. For instance, a Whippet will be much more sensitive than a Staffordshire Bull Terrier. Touch is a very important sense to the dog, and he should not be deprived of the chance to interact with other canines and humans – as long as he knows the rules.

EXTRA-SENSORY PERCEPTION

There has always been a lot of argument about whether or not dogs have psychic powers, extra-sensory perception, a sixth sense, clairvoyance, or whatever you like to call it. Even the sceptics have to admit that there are some actions dogs take that are incomprehensible to humans.

How do you explain the story about a pack of West Country Foxhounds who started to 'sing' in their kennel when their late Master's coffin was being lowered into the grave in a churchyard several miles away? Then there was the American Service Dog who, with his handler, was taken by air on a reconnaissance mission in the jungle. When the mission was ambushed, the men were taken out by air but the dog had to be left behind. No-one expected to see him again but, after three days, he was found asleep on his handler's bunk, having travelled through thirty miles of enemy-occupied, unknown jungle to get there. How? We shall never know.

Mary once worked in boarding kennel near the South Downs in southern England. When she had time off, she would take several dogs for a run on the Downs, where there was a prehistoric chalk figure. Not one dog would ever put a foot on this figure. There were many stories of dogs who, during the First World War, made their way by train and boat from Britain to France, eventually finding their way to their master in his unit at the front line. These dogs had been firmly shut up in kennel or yard when the master left and had travelled many miles before reaching the coast. During the last war, many Air Force pilots had dogs in camp with them. These dogs would wait patiently for the planes to come back. Long before the radar had picked up the returning planes, the dogs would go out to greet them, but if a plane had been shot down over Germany or France, the dog whose master had been flying it often stayed behind.

Sandra Stone, founder of the organisation Children in Hospital and Animal Therapy Association (CHATA), told us how a very boisterous Labrador, a registered CHATA dog, would play rough-and-tumble with a child who was well enough to play, but, when taken to see a seriously ill child, the same dog would hold out a paw and very gently lay his head on the bed. The charity Support Dogs have found that a number of dogs can detect the onset of an epileptic seizure half an hour or more before it happens. These dogs can be trained to alert the owner in time for the right action to be taken. How the dogs do this is unknown, although there are several theories.

Most dog owners can tell stories about their pets which defy reasoned thinking. We know dogs are very sensitive to human moods. If there is an upheaval in the family – a disruptive teenager, divorce, unemployment – the dog can develop behavioural problems. He knows something is wrong, but cannot understand what it is. Everyone is too busy trying to sort things out to bother with him, so he becomes confused.

Many things which dogs do and which their owners cannot understand are not due to ESP, but to their acute awareness of our moods and actions. Although we cannot completely understand our dogs, we can, at least, be aware of how perceptive they are, and make allowances for them when our irrational behaviour upsets them.

CHAPTER TWO

CROSSING THE DIVIDE

Communication is an essential tool in building relationships, and this applies as much in the animal world as it does among humans. As we have a complex system of verbal communication, we are less reliant on more subtle forms, such as reading body language and facial expressions, which animals use as their own form of sign language. In order to cross the divide and communicate with our dogs, we need to become more subtle in our approach and find common ground.

BODY LANGUAGE

The dog is not only an expert at using body language, he is also clever at reading it correctly in other species, including man. If we could learn to interpret his body language as well as he does ours, there would be far fewer misunderstandings between us. His dam starts to teach him body language when he is in the nest, and it is to be hoped that his owner will continue the good work by allowing him to socialise with other puppies and dogs. It is very important that, as a puppy and adolescent, he learns how to behave in the company of other dogs.

Body language is a two-way system. We need to watch our dog carefully and to make every effort to understand what he is trying to tell

A puppy is quick to learn that a cat with bristling fur is best left alone.
Photos: Steve Nash.

us. He has little trouble understanding the body language of other domestic animals, but man often seems intent on confusing him. The dog is still a predator, and, as such, must be able to grasp very quickly what his prey intends to do next. Anyone who has watched a pack of wild dogs or wolves hunting will realise that they pick their prey with great care, never move until the right moment presents itself and then work as a team to make sure of a kill. If they were unable to do this, they would starve.

Our own dogs are always brought up with various other animals. They know they have to leave the sheep alone, and that when the ewes have lambs they must be wary. An old ewe that might have allowed a young dog to wander at will around her field will, when she has lambs, be a very different animal. It takes little time for the dog to find this out; a fixed stare, a stamping hoof and threatening body stance all give out the message "Keep off".

Most of our ponies are well-behaved with dogs, but the odd one is liable to kick at a nosy one. Again, in a surprisingly short time, the dogs get to know which pony should be left alone. Cats have the dogs under control in no time. A new pup, bent on investigating this furry being, is soon taught that a cat with bristling fur and an unsheathed paw is best left alone.

Although today, the dog's senses are not so keen as those of the wolf, they are still very acute – much more so than our own. The slightest change in facial expression – a smile, raised eyebrows, a threat or laughter in the eyes, tears, a grin – all are registered by the dog very quickly. He never misses such signs, and, if we are not careful, it is all too easy to give him conflicting messages, not intentionally, but enough to cause him to wonder what we really want.

Once a dog becomes part of the family, he begins to realise that, over some things, human beings are not very bright, but he develops a sort of 'sense of feel' towards his family. He is likely to get upset if he has done nothing wrong but we shout at him to vent our frustration when we have done something really stupid. He may sneak up on the chair beside his owner without being asked, but if the owner is half-asleep and mildly mutters "Get off", he takes no notice and just curls up, but, if he has misjudged it, a look is usually enough to make him change his mind. He knows when we are upset, and many a person sitting crying has felt a cold nose pushed into their hands or a paw placed softly on a knee in sympathy. Children often find the family dog lends a more sympathetic ear than an adult, and is someone to whom they can safely tell their secrets.

READING THE SIGNS

We often have owners come to us for advice about their dogs, and many of them say "I don't know why he did it, there was no reason for it." However, there always is a reason, and once we can get an owner thinking back, it can usually be found. Either the owner did not realise the dog was warning them, or they had given him a confused signal or, sometimes, a completely wrong one. If your dog does something quite unexpected and out of character, then you must try to work out why.

Many things we never teach our dogs, they learn by experience. Mary often reads a book in the evening, and, when it is time for bed, puts the book down and takes off her reading glasses. Immediately, our dogs get up and go to the door ready for their last run – all without a word being said. If only we could pick up changes as quickly, life would be much simpler for our dogs.

Although most behaviour signs are common to all canines, some of the breeds which man has manufactured have difficulty expressing themselves in the way that they should. An Old English Sheepdog may be looking scared, submissive or dominant, but as you cannot see his eyes or his body for hair, so how can you tell? A Bloodhound may hear a sudden noise and stop and look alert – or can he? His ears are far too long and heavy to be raised. Dogs with short tails, in some breeds just stumps, can, and do, 'waggle their bums' but that is hardly the same as having a tail with which to indicate your feelings. A tail can be held high or low, stiff or slack, wag slowly, speed up, wag really fast and give off so many signals which a dog without a tail cannot really do.

A dog has no morals, and those who say their dog often looks guilty,

Body posture and expression reflect how a dog is feeling. This dog is positive and happy because it is being praised.

Downcast and forlorn, the dog receives a telling off.

as many owners do, are wrong. Let us say that the last time the owner came home, he found the dog had chewed up his slippers. If no-one has taught him not to chew slippers, how can he be expected to know it was wrong? The dog rushed to meet him with the remains in his mouth. What happened next? In all probability, the owner shouted at him, shook him, gave him a thump and threw him out in the garden. All the poor dog wanted to do was welcome him home. So, next time the owner comes back, what happens? Whether or not he has chewed anything up, he displays submission and fear, not guilt. He hears the key in the door and may run away and hide, or creep forward on his stomach, his ears laid back, and sometimes urinating at the same time, which gets him into even more trouble when he is only trying to demonstrate his submission. This is the attitude of a dog who does not know why he was punished. A dog should only be punished if he knows what he has done wrong. A dog who has been fairly corrected for a misdemeanour will usually approach his owner after a short while to make up. He will approach with a wary look in his eyes, but with his head held high, and, probably, gently wagging his tail. He might nudge his owner or offer a paw. A dog should never have to obey out of fear. A dog who has been brought up properly and who has been well disciplined will understand why he has been corrected and will accept it.

Although dogs do not think and reason in the same way that we do, we have no doubt that many of them do think and work things out for themselves. Right from birth they learn by experience, not by formal teaching. They learn that a certain action brings its own reward and is worth repeating, or that another action, such as touching an electric fence, is not so good.

We have electric fencing in the fields where the sheep are grazed. Without any help from us, the dogs soon work out not only that it is unwise to touch the fence, but also that if it is not ticking, then it will not 'bite'.

Another example of a communication misunderstanding between puppies and humans occurred when we had a girl helping in the kennels. John could not understand why a litter of Corgi pups would go into their kennel when called with the aid of food. One day he watched this girl calling them from the bottom of their large run. As she called them, she went towards them, and they all sat there and waited for her. She picked them up, a couple at a time, and took them back to their kennel. Without realising it, she had taught them that calling them meant "Sit and wait for me".

AGGRESSION AND DOMINANCE

Aggression and dominance are often confused. A dominant dog has complete confidence in himself – he does not need to be aggressive. John once had a retired Royal Air Force German Shepherd bitch who had been trained to attack. Her name was Agate, and she had been living with a sensible family, where she enjoyed playing with the children, who were very fond of her. Unfortunately, the family were

A growl and an open stare.

The mouth is open showing bared teeth, and the ears are erect.

Tense and threatening, the teeth are bared, and the corners of the mouth are drawn forward.

moving and could not take her with them, which upset both the family and the bitch. However, she had a good life with us, and we used her on displays of police work. John used to take her everywhere with him, and, more than once, when he was waiting at a bus stop, someone nearby would move away, asking "Is that dog safe?" The answer was that she was, as long as no-one threatened her owner. But Agate would fix a stranger with her eyes, and just stand and stare at them, which always made them feel uncomfortable. She would never have bitten, however, unless provoked, and was certainly not aggressive.

Another good example of dominance was a Maremma Sheepdog called Jason we once had. At that time we had a mixed pack of dogs, and we used them for film and television work. John was in London, working on a film, and had Jason and a tiny Papillon called Tiggy running around in Hyde Park. Tiggy had ventured rather far afield when a large, standard brown Poodle appeared and ran towards her. She panicked, and ran back towards John. Jason, who was our undisputed pack leader at home, immediately ran forward, and Tiggy ran in behind him. Jason just stopped and stood still. He was a big, imposing dog, and he pulled himself up to his full height, raised his head and his tail and just stared at the Poodle. The latter ground to a halt, gradually dropped his eyes and his tail, tried to make himself as small as possible, slowly turned round, and slunk off. No growling, no snarling; just a dominant dog using the right body language to say "Leave her alone or else." Dogs, as a rule, do not want to fight. In the wild, a confrontation is always avoided if possible. Fighting weakens the pack. If the Poodle had not understood Jason's body language, then the outcome could have been very different.

NERVOUSNESS AND RESERVE

A natural reserve, often seen in some breeds and in some individuals, is very often mistaken for nervousness, but the two are very different. As we keep saying, dogs and people can be very similar. Some people are "Hail fellow, well met" types, whilst others are more reserved and take time to make friends. Dogs are exactly the same. A nervous dog may react in several ways. If on a lead and unable to escape from the perceived threat, the dog may crouch down, hide behind the owner, tail down and ears back, or he may whimper or urinate if he is really worried. If in the house and afraid of strangers, he will probably yap and bark hysterically, and, if approached, dash for the nearest cover and stay there, whining or growling

The head is lowered and the ears are flat.

nervously. He will not allow anyone to touch him. If cornered, he may well bite out of fear.

A reserved dog who has been properly socialised behaves quite differently. He will not willingly approach a stranger, but will usually allow a stranger to stroke him but show no response. He prefers to be left alone, and will often ignore people he does not know. We once had a Saluki named Fahmi, who was one of our team of demonstration dogs and a fantastic jumping dog. Noise, traffic, bands, crowds – they never worried him. He would follow Mary anywhere without a lead, through a fairground if need be. If people reached out their hands to stroke him – he was a handsome hound – he just kept walking. If

The corners of the mouth and the lips are drawn back.

A litter of puppies will often display different characteristics. The bolder pups will be the first to investigate, while the timid will hang back.

someone came to talk to Mary and tried to pet him, he would just step aside and ignore them. Nearly everyone who met him commented that it was a pity that he was so nervous. Fahmi was not nervous at all, but it was difficult to make people understand that.

The reserved dog is very unlikely to bite, but the nervous dog sometimes has little choice. To him, strangers are a threat. He warns them to leave him alone with his body language and often by vocalising, but there is always a so-called dog-lover who thinks that he will not be bitten. As he approaches, the nervous dog warns again that he does not want to be touched, but, if his space is invaded, he inevitably will. This is an action which, in today's anti-dog world, could easily cost him his life, when all he has done is try to make his position clear.

Some dogs, usually the submissive ones, seem to grin – they pull their lips back in what could almost be called embarrassment. This usually happens when the dog meets a friend, when playing, or when the dog is not quite sure if he has done the right thing. Once the dog finds that this amuses the owner, he often does it more frequently or even on command, but many people think he is snarling and accuse him of being savage.

INTELLIGENCE

None of the dog's characteristics is as frequently misunderstood as intelligence. Generally speaking, if a dog does what the owner wants, he is considered intelligent; but if he will not, then he is stupid! In fact, owners who think that way usually have not bothered to train their dog, or have failed to teach the dog what is wanted, but are too stupid to realise it!

The wolf is a very intelligent animal. It uses this intelligence for two main purposes – to find and catch food, and to evade capture or destruction by its enemies. The dog has inherited a high level of intelligence, but it is not generally realised that it also uses its intelligence for two purposes –

Conventional obedience can be equated to army drill – but it is not a guide to intelligence.
Photo: Steve Nash.

Intelligence is difficult to assess. Is this intelligence or training?

Photo: Arthur Sidey.

learning what its owner is trying to teach it, and to find ways of evading the owner's wishes. Intelligence does not always make a dog trainable. Many 'problem' dogs are extremely intelligent, even if the same cannot always be said of their owners!

Intelligence is difficult to assess, especially on meeting a dog for the first time. Scientists conduct all sorts of tests to assess the IQ of various dogs, but these tests are conducted under controlled conditions, which are not always applicable to dogs living under what we would call normal conditions.

Magazines and, sometimes, the national newspapers print tables showing the comparative intelligence of various breeds. One of these, we found, had been compiled by an instructor at an obedience training class. He based his findings on each breed's wins in competitions, which certainly did not show much intelligence on his part. Top of the list was the Border Collie, with the Afghan at the bottom. We wonder how many Afghans he had studied for his survey? Obedience competitions do not test the dog's intelligence, they test his willingness to obey simple commands. With the exception of the retrieve and scent discrimination, all the obedience exercises are negative. Teaching a dog to walk to heel or to stay on the sit or down is really teaching him not to run off and enjoy himself. Standard obedience exercises can be compared to drill sessions in the Army – essential if men are to respond instantly and accurately to a wide range of commands. But there are few who would claim that the best man on the parade ground would automatically be the best soldier on the battlefield.

Of the hundreds of dogs we have had during the past fifty years, two stand out in memory as the least intelligent. Both were Border Collie bitches, and both were excellent sheepdogs and had won in trials. One of the most intelligent, on the other hand, was our Saluki, Fahmi, who had no desire whatsoever to become an obedience champion, although he did miss qualifying as a Companion Dog in working trials by only one point. On a sunny day, Fahmi would take his blanket out of his kennel into the run, where he would lie down on it. Now that is what we call intelligence. He had never been taught to do it, nor had he seen another dog doing it – he did it entirely of his own accord, which raises the question of whether dogs are capable of reasoning, a topic over which there are many arguments. Did Fahmi find out by accident that if he took his blanket out of his kennel, it was more comfortable to lie on than bare concrete? Or did he reason to himself that the concrete would be more comfortable if he took his blanket out to lie on? We believe he did reason, to some extent, but there are scientific types who will say it happened by accident. If it was purely accidental, it certainly showed great intelligence, as he repeated the action whenever there was a warm, sunny day.

Apart from the two very stupid Border Collies I have mentioned, we have had others of the breed who have had quite remarkable intelligence. One of these was Floss, John's dog when he worked as a shepherd and cattleman on his father's farm. One day, he saw a ewe with a lamb at the far end of a 40 acre field. Ewes with young lambs will seldom move for a dog, but John thought he would give it a try before walking all that way to see if all was well, so he sent Floss, who ran around the ewe and stopped behind her. On command, she then walked on, steadily 'eyeing' the sheep. Sheep will move more readily for some dogs than for others; this is known as 'power' in sheepdog circles, and Floss had lots of it. The ewe stamped her foot, snorted in defiance and refused to move. Then Floss did something she had never done before in her life – she barked at the sheep, which caused the ewe to put her head down and charge the dog, who took evasive action by running away. Floss then stopped and barked again at the sheep, which attacked again. Of course, Floss was taking the ewe away from where John was standing, and it soon looked as if he would have to walk further than if he had gone up there in the first place.

Then Floss suddenly changed her tactics so that she was between the ewe and her boss. She continued to bark at it and run away, but this time the ewe was heading in the right direction. Eventually, they reached John, by which time the ewe was so furious that she did not seem to notice he was there, and he simply reached down and grabbed her by the horn.

Here we have a dog with a very strong instinct to herd – to bring the sheep to the handler. Her training had been designed to strengthen that instinct, but she abandoned her training and her instinct and, instead of fetching the sheep, she allowed it to chase her in the direction she wanted it to go. When, subsequently, a ewe with a lamb faced Floss, she did not try to fetch it in the usual fashion; she teased it by barking and persuaded it to go in the direction she wanted.

There is little doubt that Floss started barking at the ewe in exasperation, but, the question is, did she work out an alternative way of getting it to move in the direction she wanted, even though it was contrary to her instinct and training? Floss could be taught to do most things a dog could be expected to do, but obviously she could not talk, so she could not tell us! We believe that both Floss and Fahmi did reason, to some extent, but there are those who disagree.

Of one thing we feel certain – that only a minority of dogs are capable of that sort of behaviour. Many dogs are very confused by owners who believe that their dog can reason; all training must be based on the assumption that dogs do not reason, even if, at times, we feel certain that they do.

INTERPRETING SOUND

We know that dogs communicate with each other and with other species using both body and vocal language. How we communicate with our dogs vocally can make a great deal of difference to the relationship we have with them.

The dog's sense of hearing is very acute, so there is seldom any need to shout at him. If you make a habit of speaking quietly, you can raise your voice in the case of an emergency, which should make the dog take notice immediately. If you spend all day shouting at him, he will just become used to the noise.

Some trainers use so-called 'silent whistles'. These are very high-pitched, and we have found that dogs with sensitive hearing can easily become upset and confused by them. We once had a Border Collie bitch, who, when she heard the whistle, very much gave the impression that the high-pitched noise hurt her ears.

Words do not matter to a dog – sounds do. It is just as easy to teach a dog to lie down by using the word "Stand" or by blowing a whistle as it is by saying "Down". Owners who think that their dog understands every word they say are mistaken – the dog understands the sounds you make and the tone of your voice.

Being pack animals, dogs like to join in any activity involving their own family 'pack'. If, for instance, children are running around, playing a ball game and shouting, the family dog will almost certainly want to join in and will bark excitedly. It is a natural reaction. If you are out for

Pups will learn to respond to any sound they associate with reward.
Photo: Sally Anne Thompson.

This sheepdog has learnt to respond to another sound, in this case, a whistle.
Photo: Keith Allison.

a walk and you pass a school playground during play time, there will be a lot of rushing about and excitement. Your dog may want to join in this too, but in this case he cannot be allowed to do so. If he starts barking, do not shout at him; he will simply think that you are joining in the fun. Instead, tell him quietly to stop and walk him past. If he does not calm down, keep walking past, correcting him when he barks and praising him when he is quiet; he will soon get fed up!

In training animals, almost any sounds can be used. One modern method is the use of a 'clicker', a small gadget held in the hand, which clicks when pressed and gains the dog's attention. John once knew a very successful obedience trainer and competitor who used the rattle of a chain in her pocket to the same effect.

Animals will respond to almost any sound they associate with something pleasant or unpleasant. Dolphins and performing whales are trained using clickers or whistles. Chickens come to the rattling of a bucket; cows rush to the gate when they hear the tractor bringing their feed; fish have been taught to rise to the surface at the sound of a bell being rung. Our sheep, on hearing the feed bins in the barn being opened, rush to their feeding troughs. They mix happily with our own dogs, but at the sound of a strange bark, rush to the other end of the field.

All dogs should associate the sound of their own name with pleasure, but they respond with fear to a sound they associate with a bad experience. A dog involved in a traffic accident may be afraid of the sound of screeching brakes. Our own Chihuahua, usually a bold little dog, was once accidentally hit on the head by a seat belt buckle being released. Now, she jumps every time the belt is released and she hears the recoil.

Sheepdog trainers often use whistles, as the sound can be heard at a distance better than the human voice can. Also, if a dog is used to a certain set of whistles, it is easier to work him if he changes owners.

Strangers with harsh voices, however friendly they mean to be, can intimidate nervous dogs. Someone with a soft, quiet voice will often make friends with the same dog right away. A dog, especially a dominant one, who refuses to obey one member of the family who keeps 'asking' him to do something will respond differently when another family member 'tells' him, in a firm tone, what is wanted.

Dogs enjoy being talked to. Some modern training methods do not use the voice at all during the course of the training programme; we consider this to be a great mistake. Dogs communicate with each other vocally, and, to get the best out of your dog, we are sure that you need to talk to him, and you will both enjoy it.

CHAPTER THREE

THE PACK INSTINCT

No animal has been trained to carry out as many different tasks for the benefit of man as the dog. It is commonly believed that the reason why the dog is so trainable is because of his superior intelligence. That is not so. In fact, exceptional intelligence in a dog can, and sometimes does, make him very difficult to train – especially when combined with a stupid owner!

THE PACK LEADER

The domestic cat is every bit as intelligent as its canine counterpart, but it cannot be taught to do many of the things which a dog can. This is because it has no pack instinct. Cat lovers often prefer cats to dogs because of their independence, which, of course, is why they are so difficult to train – although they can be trained to a much greater degree than is generally believed.

In the wild, dogs live in a well-organised pack with a well-defined hierarchy and a leader at the top. Cats, on the other hand, are usually solitary animals. A dominant cat in a group is not obeyed; the others just keep out of its way.

Dogs enjoy helping their owners in many ways.

Photo: Brian McGovern.

Fortunately for us, the dog is willing, even anxious, to accept a person as a pack leader. It is worth noting at this stage that none of the many tasks which dogs carry out so successfully can be performed without the help of a human leader, which is why those who aspire to training a dog and having an enjoyable relationship with it must understand the role of pack leader. There is no need to behave exactly like a dog, but it is important to understand how dogs behave towards other members of the pack, and particularly how a bitch trains her puppies and how the leader controls his pack. Most people understand that the pack leader is the dominant member of the pack, but there is much misunderstanding about dominance, which is often confused with aggression. Some dominant dogs are aggressive but they are not the best pack leaders.

For many years, we kept a 'pack' of 20 to 25 dogs which were trained for film and television work. We had many different breeds, so it was not an orthodox pack as would be found in the wild, but they did exercise and work together, and they sorted out their own hierarchy. They did not choose their leader; it was our job to fill that role to the best of our ability. This was made easier by the fact that there was nearly always a canine 'second in command'.

Over a period of some 50 years, we had a number of leaders, and it was interesting to observe the difference in behaviour between them. If a leader was absent, for whatever reason, there was usually a period of unrest within the pack, during which time we had to be much more careful in keeping order. Quite often, however, a younger dog had been assessing the situation for some time, and was only too eager to fill the vacancy. Sometimes two, or even three, would want the job, leading to fighting. We had to make it very clear that, even if the canine leader had gone, there was still a two-legged leader in overall charge.

The various leaders showed varying degrees of aggression and frequently made efforts to impress on members of the pack that they must not get above their status. One of our very best leaders was the big Maremma dog called Jason, whom we mentioned earlier. He was a very competent and confident leader, and, like all good leaders, he had no need to throw his weight around. A look was enough to stop any trouble from developing. As a youngster he was very dominant and, as he matured, he challenged John for leadership several times. In those days, John was younger and fitter and soon sorted him out, after which he was never any trouble.

In the wolf pack, the leader, or 'alpha male', usually has one or two 'assistants'. These are younger males who may one day challenge him and take over his position, but, until that happens, the leader keeps law and order throughout the pack. He starts by warning the culprit with his body language, especially facial expressions, and by growling. This usually has the desired effect, but, if not, he applies some very definite positive correction, and that is that!

THE ALPHA FEMALE

Within the wolf pack, there is also an alpha female, who is treated with great respect by other pack members. She is usually the only one to have pups, which are sired by the alpha male. All members of the pack help to rear the litter;

A bitch will discipline a puppy, which will teach him the correct social behaviour.

sometimes females who are not even in whelp will produce milk and suckle the pups. As the pups grow, other members of the pack play with them and discipline them. Often one or more pack members will be left to 'baby-sit' while the pack goes off hunting.

When a female plays with her cubs, they are allowed to bite, but not too hard. If a pup's hold on its mother's ears begins to hurt, she first of all growls, which is often sufficient to make the pup release his hold. If one does not let go, the growl becomes louder and is immediately followed by a sharp snap. This frightens the pup more than it hurts him, and he may well run off yelping, as if it had been severely bitten. In a very short time, he will return to his mother, who will then caress him by licking him. The pup very soon learns to associate the growl with correction, and is careful not to bite too hard. This is a simple example of how, in the natural state, a pup is corrected for doing what he should not do and rewarded for doing what he should. Other animals discipline their offspring in a similar way. In a nature programme we were watching on television, a group of baboons were travelling along a track in the forest. Several of the females were carrying young ones on their backs. One baby jumped off onto the ground. Without so much as a pause, its mother scooped it up in one hand, shook it, and threw it over her shoulder on to her back. The infant did not jump off again!

Most of the higher animals discipline their offspring to a greater or lesser degree, and we believe that it is natural and right. In recent years, these principles have lost favour within society, not only in the way we discipline our dogs, but also in the way we discipline our children. We make no claims to be child experts, nor do we have any intention of giving advice on the subject. Our reason for mentioning it is because we believe that attitudes about dogs are very similar to attitudes about children.

TRAINING

In the past, dogs were often, though not always, trained by methods

These dogs are enjoying a walk with their human pack leader.
Photo: Sally Anne Thompson.

which today would be considered harsh or even cruel. We are delighted that these methods have, to a great extent, though not entirely, been replaced by methods which are more humane and usually more successful. However, much as we welcome this change, it does appear that the pendulum has swung, and continues to swing, too far in the opposite direction. Old-fashioned correction and reward have been replaced by positive and negative reinforcement. It is now considered unkind, if not positively cruel, to make a dog do something the owner wants him to do or, more importantly, to stop him doing something the dog wants to do. One very well-known behaviourist wrote a book on training with the subtitle "Never say No". His advice on teaching the "down" command is to wait until the dog lies down of its own accord – termed 'negative reinforcement'. As it lies down, the advice is to give the command "down". Immediately the dog lies down, praise lavishly – 'positive reinforcement'. By repeating this process, the dog should eventually lie down in response to the command. For those with time to spare, or who have a lethargic dog that enjoys lying down, this may be fine, but we do not all have the time to spare, and some dogs are reluctant to lie down if there is something more interesting to do.

We know that dogs can and have been trained without any correction, but we also know owners who have tried and failed using the same method. We cannot accept that it is unkind to treat an animal in a manner similar to the way its own mother would treat it. Indeed, we go further, believing that it can be unkind not to treat a puppy according to the principles its mother would adopt, even if the method of applying these principles may be different. Many dogs are euthanised as a result of behaviour problems simply because their owners adhered to the "never say no" principle.

The mind of the wolf is programmed to enable it to live as a member of a pack and to obey the rules of that pack, whatever his position in the hierarchy. To rebel against these rules has very drastic consequences, including expulsion or death.

The domestic dog accepts man as a leader – providing he behaves like a leader! During thousands of years of domestication, dogs have been bred for specific purposes. For most of these, it was essential that the dog was amenable to training. Any that were too difficult or impossible to train would have been discarded. The result is that, with few exceptions, the majority of dogs of all breeds actually want someone to tell them what to do. This brings us to the question of dominance, a subject which was unknown until the advent of the behaviourist movement. In the first edition of "The Family Dog", written by John in 1957, he did not mention the word dominance, but today's behaviour counsellors maintain that dominance is the cause of more behaviour problems than all other causes. That may well be, but true canine dominance is frequently confused with human aggression.

WHO IS DOMINANT?

Dominance is relative. It is a fact accepted by people who have spent much of their lives working with animals that it is quite common for an animal to behave in a dominant manner towards one person, but to be completely submissive to another. This is particularly applicable to dogs, and it is not uncommon to find a dog that obeys certain members of a family but has no respect for others, which shows that some members of the family are more dominant than others. Therein lies the

answer as to why dominance, which was no problem 30 years ago, is a big problem today. It is not because dogs have become more dominant than they were in the past, but because a high percentage of dog owners are wimps who allow themselves to be bossed about by their own young children and their dogs!

Puppies should be groomed from an early age. It teaches them to be submissive, and strengthens the bond with the owner.
Photo: Sally Anne Thompson.

Behaviour counsellors have benefited from this, but we have some difficulty in understanding the advice that some of them offer. It is very important, they say, to act the part of the pack leader right from the start, but an eight-week-old puppy, in a strange environment, does not want a leader – he wants his mother! This is why women make much better puppy-rearers than men. Even so, we feel that many, if not most, problems are due either to failure to apply correction, or to failure to apply it at the right time. We also know that some advocates of reward-only training do not always practise what they preach!

As we have already said, dominance is often confused with aggression, but there are many examples of the one being present without the other, and also examples of the two being combined, which usually leads to trouble. One of the first signs of aggressive dominance appears when the puppy guards his food. Many owners regard it as natural, overlooking the fact that many actions which are perfectly natural are neither desirable nor permissible in today's society. However, this is not the main issue – the problem is not that the puppy guards his food, which is only natural to some puppies, but that, in most cases, he gets away with it. If your puppy growls or curls his lip as you reach towards his food and you withdraw your hand, you have issued a clear signal that he is superior to you, so the pup says to himself "Well, that was easy, I'll try it again." So he does, and, if the same thing happens, it gives him great confidence and he quickly decides that if there is anything he does not want you to have, all he has to do is growl and pull a funny face and you do not have it. It may start with his food bowl, but can quickly extend to toys, the rug, a favourite chair, even your bed. It is quite astonishing the number of people, sometimes even 'macho' men, who have told us that their puppy will not let them touch his bed, food bowl or whatever. An eight-week-old puppy, a canine infant – the mind boggles!

A good example of where this can lead was a couple we heard of who had a Cocker Spaniel who, if it felt that way inclined (and it often did), would lie on the mat by the front door. While he was there, neither the husband nor the wife were allowed to go in or out of the front door.

The Pack Instinct

We make a practice of stroking a puppy when he is feeding, or at least when he starts to feed. He must be taught, right from the start, that any member of the family has the right to go to him and remove his bowl when he is feeding if they so wish. We usually make a puppy sit, put his dish on the ground and make him wait until we say he can have it. If you then stroke him gently and talk to him most pups will be so busy eating that they will not even notice. If he does growl, you should immediately growl back "No", grasp him firmly but gently by the scruff of the neck in one hand and take the bowl away with the other. Make him sit, and, once he is calm, praise him and put his dish down again. Stroke him again, and, if he behaves, drop a liver treat in his bowl. Once he accepts the stroking, take his bowl away, make him sit again and give it back to him with a little extra in it. It is always important that a puppy or dog should allow someone near his food, especially if children are around.

A puppy who does not respond to this treatment is either very aggressive by nature (making it all the more necessary to show him who is boss), or he has previously been allowed to get away with it.

Here it is worth remembering that short-tempered people very seldom have dominant or aggressive dogs. We are certainly not referring to a bad or an uncontrollable temper, but to a quick temper. This is the sort of person who, when a puppy snaps at his hand, does not stand there wondering what to do, or go looking for a newspaper to roll up, look up what to do in a book or ring a behaviour counsellor! We mean the sort of person who smacks the puppy across the face as he tries to bite, which will not hurt the pup, but it will give him a mighty fright. It is very much the same treatment that his mother would apply, using her mouth instead of a hand. Even an aggressive puppy is unlikely to do the same thing again in a hurry.

Unless this tendency to guard is corrected as it appears, it will almost certainly create a problem. As the pup grows, so does the problem. In many cases, it increases so much that the dog becomes dangerous and is euthanised – as a result of being allowed to do something which is 'natural'.

HOW MANY DOGS?

Although seldom referred to as such, humans have a pack instinct very similar to that of the dog. We have a similar hierarchy and even talk of 'top dogs' and 'underdogs'. While the majority of people are quite happy to be led, there are many others continuously struggling to be top dogs. There are, too, just as many trying by fair means or foul to knock the top dogs off their pedestals in the hope of taking over their

Although this pack has established its own hierarchy, the huntsman is still 'top dog'. Each hound is called individually by name to go and feed.

This puppy enjoys playing with his older friend, but it is important for the owner to play with him too.

positions. A gang of schoolchildren will get up to all sorts of mischief which none of them would consider doing on their own. Likewise, two dogs who are unlikely to get into any trouble as individuals can present a very different picture if they pal up and form a pack. One might expect two dogs to be twice as difficult to control as either of the dogs on his own, but in fact they will be a great deal more difficult than that, because the hunting instinct strengthens the pack instinct.

This affects the pet dog owner in different ways. Many dogs are perfectly happy to stay on their own ground and will not go out of the garden gate even if it is left open, but, if the same dog pals up with the dog next door, there is every likelihood that the two will go off together. The trouble that two perfectly well-behaved dogs can get up to together is inestimable.

Many people keep two dogs in the belief that they will be company for each other in the owner's absence. This is a very good idea, and one which we practise ourselves. It is all very well saying that a dog should never be left on its own, but, much as a dog adds (or should add) to the quality of life of its owner, there are few people able or willing to devote their whole lives to a dog. In any case, the dog is usually far happier pottering about – or lying in the sun or shade as he chooses – in the garden than being dragged around the streets, tied up outside shops or left to bake in a stationary car. Two dogs will be even happier, and take more exercise playing together in a limited space in half an hour than one dog taken out on a lead for an hour or more. However, there are several problems to be guarded against when two dogs share a household. Firstly, there is the probability that they will form their own pack. Instead of accepting you and building up a rapport with you as leader, one of them will adopt the position of leader and the other will be his 'servant'. This is likely to happen when two puppies are purchased together. They become very good friends, and the more dominant one becomes the leader, and the other the follower. This means that you are liable to end up as something that supplies this pack with food and a comfortable bed!

Our advice is not to start with two puppies of the same age. Whether or not they are from the same litter, the chances are they will form a stronger bond with each other than with you. Start with one puppy, and wait until he becomes attached to you before acquiring another.

Some people who have a bitch decide that it would be nice to breed a litter and keep one of the pups, but unless an effort is made to transfer the puppy's affection from its mother to you, the natural bond is liable to become stronger as the pup gets older. We have found that this applies to male puppies more than to their sisters, but that is a personal observation, not a scientific fact. The risk of this happening can be reduced by treating the pup as an individual. Take him out on his own – play with him and give him some basic training away from his mother. It is a good idea to let him sleep separately from his mother, in another room or in a crate.

Many people worry when an old dog begins to show his age and they start to think about a replacement. Should they get a puppy or wait until the old dog has gone? This question usually arises because of concern that the old dog might resent a newcomer in the household. Well, he might, but in nearly all cases we have known, the old dog has taken on a new lease of life. We are talking about a reasonably healthy old dog here, and not one that is actually dying.

Care should always be taken when introducing a puppy to an old dog – or to any adult dog, for that matter. You should allow them to do this themselves, rather than try to make them be friends. Never make the old dog feel that you are protecting the puppy. If the pup is over-exuberant and the old dog growls, or even snaps at him, just let them get on with it. The old dog is simply teaching the youngster to respect his elders and betters. He needs to learn what a growl means and will respond by adopting a submissive attitude, turning his head away, rolling on his back and so on.

Very occasionally an adult dog will seriously attack and injure a puppy. Such dogs are over-aggressive and are usually known to fight with other dogs. This is often because they were not socialised with other dogs as puppies and never had the chance to learn correct canine behaviour. If you know such a dog, never try to introduce a puppy to him.

CHAPTER FOUR

THE HUNTING INSTINCT

As previously mentioned, there is much evidence to suggest that the first practical use to which man put the dog was to help him catch his food. Not only did he encourage and probably train dogs to hunt, he bred dogs to hunt even better than their wild ancestors. Long before Mendel and his theories on genetics, it would appear that man adhered to the rule of 'like begets like'. If someone had a bitch which was a very good hunting dog, they would look around for an equally good or even better dog to mate her with. By this simple process, the hunting instinct in the domestic dog has become even stronger than in its wild ancestors. A wolf hunts when it is hungry, and, when it catches its prey, it eats as much as it can and then rests to digest what it has eaten. It does not hunt again until it is hungry.

MAN'S HUNTING INSTINCT

Many domestic dogs will chase even when they have just had a meal – perhaps not as successfully, but equally enthusiastically. A Greyhound will chase a dummy hare around a racetrack once or twice a week without ever catching it! This is the result of careful selective breeding for a certain purpose, or even specialist branches of the same common purpose.

So we have dogs bred to hunt by sight, such as Salukis and Greyhounds, and ones bred to hunt by scent, such as Bloodhounds and Foxhounds. We have breeds which have been bred to hunt but which can still be kept under control, and breeds which are simply bred to hunt. For instance, once a Greyhound or Saluki has 'taken off' after a hare it is difficult – usually impossible – to stop it. A Spaniel, on the other hand, will push a rabbit out of a bush, then sit down and watch it run away. This is due firstly to training, but also to the breeding of dogs which can be trained to respond in this manner. It would be more than unusual to find a Greyhound or any other sight hound that could be taught to do this.

Although man no longer has to hunt to survive, the hunting instinct in the human race is as strong as ever. At first glance, this may not appear to be the case. The big game hunter's gun has been replaced by a camera; instead of wild animal trophies to hang on the wall, the photographer brings back pictures and film which is sometimes shown on television so that we can all enjoy it. Nevertheless, the wildlife

The Greyhound has been selectively bred to hunt by sight, and an artificial lure is sufficient stimulus.

Photo: Steve Nash.

photographer is still a hunter, using all the hunting instincts of primitive man in search of food.

No pack of hounds in pursuit of a fox shows more aggression and enthusiasm than a pack of reporters and photographers in pursuit of a celebrity. They show no mercy or consideration for their 'prey' nor for each other. 'Cops and Robbers', either real or imaginary, have always fascinated people of all ages, thanks to our instinct to pursue and catch a 'quarry'.

The most extreme example of the human hunting instinct – which frequently gets out of control – is to be seen amongst the very people who want to ban hunting. The hunt saboteurs and other activists pursue their prey (those who hunt) with an enthusiasm and viciousness seen in neither the people nor the hounds they are hunting. In pursuit of their cause they see no harm in injuring or even killing both people and animals. Horses have been injured and hounds blinded or killed by saboteurs.

INSTINCT AND THE PET

We do believe that the hunting instinct is as strong, or even stronger, in the human animal than in the dog, yet people who have kept dogs all their lives will wonder why their dog, who they think would not hurt a fly, chases the neighbour's cat. To most present-day dog owners, their dog's hunting instinct is rarely an asset, and is frequently a liability. Nearly all cases of livestock worrying, car chasing and, often, children being bitten by dogs, result from the hunting instinct. It is present in every breed, although sometimes lacking in an individual animal.

Fortunately, there is another side to this picture. Few people today rely on their dogs to catch their dinner, but the hunting instinct is still useful for many other purposes. There are hundreds of different breeds of domestic dog throughout the world, ranging from the giant Wolfhound to the tiny Chihuahua. Looking at all these different breeds, it is difficult to believe that they all have a common ancestor – the wolf. However, if we compare the behaviour of domestic dogs of all breeds with that of the wolf, we find many similarities. Failure to appreciate this basic fact is the cause of many dog problems.

ABSENCE OF INSTINCT

Instinct could be termed a driving force which makes an animal do something without having had any previous experience or training. The first instinct to appear in a newborn puppy is the survival instinct, which makes it squirm around until it finds a teat on which it sucks instinctively. At the same time, the dam, who may never have produced or even seen a puppy before, sets about cleaning it up and biting off the umbilical cord with amazing accuracy. This, or any other instinctive behaviour, has nothing to do with intelligence. Stupid bitches are just as good as mothers as the clever ones – sometimes better.

In breeds where caesareans are commonplace, it is not unusual to find bitches with little if any maternal instinct. This is perhaps not surprising, when you consider that the bitch has never produced a puppy naturally (and was probably not born naturally herself), but has woken up after an operation to find these squeaky wee things crawling all over her.

It is very unusual for any instinct to be completely absent, but it does happen. Occasionally, a newborn pup lacks the instinct to suck and sometimes the bitch refuses to let the puppies suck. In the wild, such puppies simply die, and, because they therefore do not propagate, there is unlikely to be a problem amongst wild dogs. It is different with domestic dogs. Few breeders will allow a puppy to die or have it destroyed, either because of sentimentality, or, more likely, because the breeder thinks it might be a good show prospect. There are people who specialise in hand-rearing orphaned puppies. To most people, this would appear to be a worthwhile and compassionate task, but what is actually happening is that these hand-reared puppies are likely to grow into adults whose offspring can only survive if also hand-reared. For this reason, these abnormalities are not uncommon amongst the domestic dog.

Occasionally, other instincts are lacking too. Although rare, it is not unknown for a sheepdog puppy, bred from generations of good workers, to show absolutely no herding instinct, but that does not pose a problem. A shepherd can simply sell such a dog to a pet home, where the working instinct is usually a disadvantage anyway.

HERDING INSTINCT

An instinct is either present or absent – it comes with the genes. It can be strengthened or weakened, but it cannot be put there or taken away. It can, however, be diverted, sometimes into quite unexpected channels. The most obvious diversion can be seen in sheepdogs, where the hunting instinct has been developed into the herding instinct. This makes the dog run around a flock of sheep and fetch them back to his handler. Some people think that this is due to the dog's exceptional intelligence; that the dog realises what the handler wants, and very kindly goes and fetches the sheep to him. This is not so. When a wolf pack hunts a caribou, the faster members of the pack pass the quarry and turn it back to the slower ones coming on behind – just like a sheepdog heading a sheep that has broken away from the flock.

Of course, a sheepdog is not supposed to attack sheep, but many do

The sheepdog is 'eyeing' a sheep.

Photo: Keith Allison.

and, without training, many more would. The majority of young sheepdogs have to be corrected for 'gripping' during their course of training. In country areas, most sheep-worrying is due to sheepdogs, and the greatest damage is caused when two or three untrained dogs form a pack and behave in a very similar way to a pack of wolves.

Instinct can be strengthened or weakened, firstly by selective breeding and secondly by use or lack of use. The herding instinct has been strengthened to such a degree that, although it is derived from the hunting instinct, most sheepdogs can fairly easily be trained to herd without attacking.

The popularity of sheepdog trials has resulted in what is virtually a new breed, known as the Border Collie. By careful selective breeding, and a good deal of inbreeding, dogs have been produced with great 'eye and style', which helps these dogs to win trials, but many of them have a quite abnormal herding instinct. They will herd anything that moves, from a cat on the hearth to a double-decker bus. John had a very well-bred, stylish working bitch who, if a log was rolled along the ground, would cast round it and take up a position at 12 o'clock. If left alone, she would stay there all day. Such behaviour is not normal, and is certainly not due to intelligence. It is, in fact, an example of how intelligence can be overruled by instinct.

Apart from its strong herding instinct, the Border Collie has been bred to respond instantly to commands. The ordinary farmer or shepherd simply sends his dog out to gather a flock of sheep and waits by the gate until he brings them back. The trial dog, on the other hand, is expected to manoeuvre a small group of sheep around a specially designed course. To do this, the dog must respond instantly and without question to a wide range of commands, and they have been bred for generations to do just that. A dog who thinks for himself can be an advantage on a farm but a disadvantage on the trial field.

So, the Border Collie's ability to obey commands, combined with an exceptional desire to be doing something, anything rather than nothing, has led to the breed being trained for many different purposes. It is probably the most versatile of all breeds, but the one job for which it is quite unsuitable is as a pet. It excels in obedience competitions where, with the exception of the retrieve and scent discrimination, all exercises are negative. Any attempt by the dog to think for himself is liable to incur penalties.

Many Border Collies have now been purchased as pets. Quite often the result is a disaster for both dog and owner. A frustrated Border Collie is a very unhappy animal who can quite easily go mad.

ENCOURAGING INSTINCT

As we have already said, instincts can be strengthened or weakened by selective breeding and by use or lack of use. A sheepdog puppy with a normal herding instinct is unlikely to show that instinct until 4 or 5 months of age. We have known several who showed no signs of a herding instinct until well over a year old, but who eventually became excellent workers. Quite often, the herding instinct appears suddenly and unexpectedly. A puppy may have followed the shepherd on his daily rounds without paying any attention to the sheep, but then, one day, he suddenly takes off, of his own accord, and rounds up some sheep. In sheepdog terms, this is known as 'starting to run', and until and unless

The working sheepdog should be encouraged to 'run' when the instinct shows signs of developing.

Photo: Keith Allison.

that happens, there is no point in attempting to train the dog.

The first time that the pup goes after sheep, he may do so rather hesitantly. He may run after them, then come back to his handler for reassurance that it is OK for him to do that. With encouragement, the herding instinct quickly develops. A pup who is reluctant to run can be encouraged by allowing him to follow an older, trained dog. Here, the pack instinct strengthens the herding instinct, but, if a pup will not run without an older dog, he is unlikely to be a very good worker. There is also a strong possibility that he will not run on his own, which can make him quite useless if the other dog is not there.

It is instinct, not intelligence, which makes a young sheepdog 'start to run'. Stupid dogs can be just as keen as clever ones. Once they do start, they have to be taught how to run, which side to go, to keep well back from wild sheep, close up to stubborn ones and much else. It is much easier to teach all these movements to an intelligent dog than to a stupid one.

If the dog is destined to be a sheepdog, it is important that the herding instinct is encouraged when it first appears. It will then strengthen rapidly, sometimes at an astonishing speed. If not allowed to develop, it will probably weaken and may die out altogether. Sheepdog pups brought up on farms often get into mischief – chasing or even killing hens, or just getting in the way when stock are being moved, for example. Farmers are not noted for their patience or ability to read a dog's mind, and sometimes severely punish the pup, who is only doing what comes naturally, for his mistakes. Often, a pup treated in this way refuses to round up sheep when he is expected to do so. Not only has he been cured of chasing hens, he has also been 'cured' of herding. Although it can sometimes be done, it is very difficult to arouse the herding instinct in a pup who has been treated this way.

Exactly the same applies to retrieving, another diversion of the hunting instinct. Many pups, especially of the retrieving breeds, will pick up objects and bring them to their owners without any training or encouragement, which is fine until the pup finds one of your best shoes lying on the floor. After having a good chew, he brings it to you, expecting to be praised, but what happens is that he is shouted at, told he is a bad dog and shut outside. Later on you throw a ball, which he has always been keen to retrieve. This time he may well run after it and pick it up, but will he bring it back? Not likely. He is not stupid, and knows what happened last time he brought something to you. The way to stop a puppy picking up something that you do not want him to have is to keep it out of his reach.

The age at which instincts make an appearance varies enormously between breeds and between individuals. Border Collies with an extra strong herding instinct will often show eye and herd their siblings when only five or six weeks old. Retriever pups will often pick up all sorts of objects and carry them around for no apparent reason – they just do it instinctively. It is wrong to assume that if a puppy bred for a specific purpose does not show the required instinct, he will not be any good. Our most recent example is Tolly, a Nova Scotia Duck Tolling Retriever we purchased at seven weeks old. Her breeder told us that she was sure of two things: that the pup would retrieve, and that she would be keen on swimming. Well, Tolly showed absolutely no inclination to pick up anything, and she had a complete aversion to even getting her feet wet! If a ball was thrown, she would look where it had gone but make no attempt to follow it or pick it up. One day when she was nearly five months old, she quite unexpectedly picked up a ball that had been thrown. She was immediately praised, and from retrieving a ball she quickly progressed to retrieving anything we wanted. She is now a keen retriever, and will hunt for hidden objects in thick cover and retrieve out of water.

INSTINCT AND ENVIRONMENT

Instincts are handed down from a dog's ancestors with his genes. Their development as the dog grows up depends on two factors – the initial strength of the instinct and the environment in which it is developed. The latter may depend very much on the sort of owner with whom the dog ends up.

A comparison can be made with a growing plant: it starts off as a seedling, and care must be taken not to trample on seedlings, although some can stand up to an amazing amount of abuse. This applies particularly to weed seedlings, which always seem much stronger and healthier than plants which we want to cultivate. Even so, it is usually possible to pull up, with finger and thumb, seedlings of the most obnoxious weeds, providing it is done when the seedlings first appear. Once the plant has established itself and put down roots, it can be very difficult, sometimes impossible, to eradicate. In the same way, desirable plants are much more robust once they are established. This means that those who want to take advantage of an instinct, such as herding or retrieving, must nurture it as it develops. It requires patience to wait until it is ready to develop, and powers of observation to see that it is showing signs of developing. Not everyone wants to encourage certain instincts – it is a sad fact that some of the characteristics which man has so carefully preserved and strengthened over thousands of years are now the cause of more dog problems than all other causes put together. Too many healthy dogs are euthanised every day, simply because they behave like dogs – the domestic dog which man has created for his own use. While the instincts which are wanted must be nurtured as they develop, like the desirable seedling, those that are not wanted must be suppressed during the same stage, like the weed seedling.

As a simple example, let us suppose that a dog who is normally friendly with people sees a jogger for the first time. Not having seen anyone behaving like that before, he runs after him, but soon returns to his owner. Next time he sees a jogger, he will be off the mark faster and show more enthusiasm, possibly barking at the jogger. The next time, he may even try to stop him by biting him. This has nothing to do with aggression or with the dog taking a dislike to that particular jogger. It is just the hunting instinct making a dog want to catch an 'animal' that is running away. Every time he does this sort of thing and gets away with it, the stronger the hunting instinct will become. Depending on the inherent instinct in that particular dog, it may quickly become so strong that it can only be controlled by keeping the dog on a lead. If, on the other hand, the dog is corrected the very first time he chases the jogger – not when he has returned to his owner, but when he is actually running after the jogger – he may not do it again. If he does and is corrected every time, there are very few dogs who cannot be taught to give up this behaviour. The majority will, in time, lose interest in joggers altogether. It is usually easy to nip a bad habit in the bud, but difficult – sometimes impossible – to break one once it is fully established.

SEARCH AND RESCUE

So, the herding instinct is a diversion of the hunting instinct, and not a very big one. Man has taken advantage of the dog's hunting instinct in many other ways. The most obvious can be seen in the police dog, who follows the track of a criminal and then catches him. This is exactly the same behaviour as is seen in the wolf which finds the track of its prey, follows it and eventually catches and eats it. Not, of course, that the police dog should eat the criminal! But it must be able to hold him until assistance arrives, in the form of his handler.

Another use for the hunting instinct is to be seen in Search and Rescue Dogs. These dogs have proved helpful in finding victims of bombs and earthquakes buried in rubble, and also in finding people lost in mountainous country. Hundreds of lives were saved by dogs during the Blitz in London and in other cities during the Second World War. Some of these dogs were trained and handled by their owners, who volunteered for this dangerous and often unpleasant task. We knew one of them very well – the late Margaret Griffin, who was awarded the British Empire Medal for her efforts during the London Blitz. John frequently acted as 'criminal' when she was training her German Shepherds, and learned a great deal from her. Her methods would certainly not meet with approval today. In training for rescue work the 'victim' was not armed with a bag of food, as is the practice today. He wore a padded arm, and when the dog found him, he jumped up and ran away. Not far, as he was quickly caught and had to put up quite a fight with the dog, which the dog enjoyed as a reward. Margaret did not believe in teaching 'man work' in play, as is the general practice today, and, when her dogs attacked, it was for real. Her dogs were under such complete control that if the victim was real, she simply told the dog to "Down" and it stayed down while the rescuers did their work.

The success of Margaret Griffin's training methods was proved when one of her bitches, Crumstone Irma, saved no fewer than 200 lives and was awarded the Dicken Medal (the dog's Victoria Cross). One of Irma's advantages was that she would never mark a dead body, which of course allowed the rescuers to concentrate on those still alive. On one occasion, a bomb had completely flattened a whole block of apartments. Irma methodically searched the rubble and marked several victims, who were rescued. When she marked another spot, the Air Raid Warden said there could not be anyone there. He had a complete list of all the occupants of the apartments and all had been accounted for. Margaret was not one to take no for an answer, and insisted that not only was someone buried there, but that the person was alive. In response to further argument, she asked if Irma had ever been wrong. No-one could remember her ever making a mistake, so a digger was brought in. It exposed an Anderson shelter (a reinforced steel box, big enough for several people to crawl into and lie down). In it were found a mother and two boys. Sadly, the mother was dead but the two children, one only a few weeks old and the other about two years, were alive, saved by a dog which probably hoped they would run away so that she could catch them!

Ironically, at the end of the war Margaret Griffin tried very hard to persuade the authorities to establish teams of Search and Rescue Dogs. She kept several dogs in training in the hope that they would be able to take part. Her pleas fell on deaf ears, but now we have Search and Rescue Dogs helping to find victims of disasters all over the world (see Chapter Ten: Working Dogs).

CHAPTER FIVE

THE GUARDING INSTINCT

The guarding instinct is not peculiar to dogs or the higher animals. Insects and fish protect their property and their families with a ferocity unsurpassed by any dog. Of course, man has a strong guarding instinct too, but, unlike other animals, he is not content just to protect his own property – he wants to grab other people's property as well.

ORIGINS

Packs of wolves and other wild dogs have their own territory, which they mark by urinating or defecating round the perimeter. To a member of another pack, these are 'keep out' signs, to be ignored at his own risk. Somewhere within that territory is the den where cubs are reared and which forms the headquarters of the whole pack. The nearer an intruder gets to the den, the more ferociously he is likely to be attacked.

It is likely that some of the cubs which primitive man captured and tamed would come to regard his cave as their den and would try to keep strangers away from it, whether on two legs or four. This instinct, passed down from the wolf to the domestic dog, has proved invaluable to man right up to the present day. As with other instincts, man has, by careful, selective breeding, produced breeds with a much stronger guarding instinct than that of their wild ancestors. He has also produced breeds with a weaker guarding instinct, but in all breeds the strength of the instinct varies enormously between individuals.

GUARDING YOUR HOME

The vast majority of dogs will make some attempt to guard their own homes – don't expect a dog to show signs of guarding until he has had time to accept that your home is also his home. That takes much longer with some dogs than with others. Puppies usually show little inclination to guard until they begin to feel 'grown up', and the age at which that happens varies, too.

Your dog should be encouraged to bark when someone knocks on the door, but he must not be allowed to keep on barking. A common mistake is to yell at the dog to be quiet, which makes him think that you are joining in, so he barks all the more. If, when you open the door, he rushes out and barks behind the caller, he is quite useless as a guard. If the caller has any evil intentions, he can easily push you into the house and shut the door in the dog's face.

Before opening the door, you should make the dog lie down beside you. It does not really matter whether he is lying, sitting or standing,

The vast majority of dogs, even small ones, will guard their owner or their property.

so long as he stays with you, but we have found that most dogs are more likely to stay in the down position. A caller who has heard a dog barking behind a door is unlikely to try to pass when he sees the dog lying quietly beside its owner, looking straight at him. The dog may have no intention of protecting you, but he will almost certainly stare at the caller. To anyone who does not know the dog, that can be quite off-putting. If you have a fairly big dog, you may prefer to have him standing beside you while you hold his collar. This can give the impression that you are holding on to the dog to make sure that he does not attack the caller.

The dog must not only be under control; he must also appear to be under control, and he must not keep on barking. There is nothing more annoying than trying to have a conversation with someone while their dog persists in barking continuously – with interruptions when the owner yells at him to shut up. This can become a very objectionable habit, and it may be worth enlisting the help of a friend to help you give the dog some lessons. Have the dog on a lead and, when the friend knocks at the door, allow him to bark and praise him for doing so. Take him to the door, on the lead and, when you get there tell him to be quiet. If he does not stop when told, tell him again, simultaneously giving him a jerk on the lead. This should stop the next bark and, once you are sure he has stopped, you can reward him. Alternatively, you can grab him around the muzzle and hold his mouth shut for a few seconds, telling him to be quiet; again, wait until he is quiet before rewarding him. Do not open the door until he is behaving quietly.

If your dog resents strangers coming into the house, try to get some help from a friend who does not know your dog, but who does understand dogs. Make sure your helper has some tidbits, and get them to knock on the door, treating the dog exactly as before. Make sure the dog is sitting quietly beside you, so that your helper can offer him a treat. It is also useful to teach a dog to shake hands with visitors. The idea is to impress on the dog that it is fine for him to bark at someone knocking on the door, but, if you say that it is OK, then he must realise that person can come in.

GUARDING CARS

Many, in fact most, dogs guard their own car. When we earned our living in the entertainment business, all our dogs had to be friendly with all and sundry. One of our very best film dogs was Tuck, a Border Collie. In the studio she was everybody's friend, but, if an artist who had been working with her in the studio went up to chat to her when she was left in the car in the car park, he/she was in for a big surprise. She really was a very keen guard and obviously meant business. In spite of our efforts to explain why she did this, few of them ever understood. We hope that readers of this book will understand that she was simply guarding what she considered to be her own and her owner's property.

In these days of car theft, a dog who guards a car can be a great asset. Even a small dog barking can attract attention which a car thief does not want, but no dog should be allowed to bark at everyone it sees. A dog should give a warning bark only when someone comes right up to the car. A dog who keeps on barking when left in a car, regardless of any threat to the car, is not guarding, but just being a nuisance. A dog barking at passers-by or other cars when the owner is driving is quite inexcusable but, unfortunately, a common sight. Like all bad habits, this dangerous one should be nipped in the bud very quickly.

A dog will guard a small space more enthusiastically than a large one. When we ran boarding kennels, it was not uncommon to put a very friendly dog into a kennel and go back in a short time to find him threatening anyone who approached him. Many boarding kennel owners have had similar experiences, and some dogs can be very menacing.

If the kennel door is opened, such a dog will usually come out and, in many cases, be just as friendly as he was before he was put in the kennel. The reason for his behaviour is that the dog, already somewhat worried at being in strange surroundings, has adopted the kennel as his new 'den', which he wants to protect.

GUARDING PROPERTY

The instinct to protect his property or possessions can lead to trouble if your dog decides that a certain armchair is just the place for him to sleep, and he does not want to share! Here we have a typical example of dominance, often made worse by an owner who stands staring at the dog trying to persuade him to leave the chair. Worse still is the owner who shouts and threatens the dog. A dominant dog is very likely to accept that as a challenge, to which he will reply. If this is a problem with your dog, and you reach out with your hand and he snaps at it, do not draw back. That will simply confirm to the dog that he is the boss, and create a situation which will rapidly become worse. If you are afraid of being bitten, which is very unlikely on the first occasion, put on a thick leather gardening glove, then take hold of the dog by the collar or scruff, pull him out of the chair and sit down in it. Let him know you are angry, but do not overdo it. You want to let him know that you are unimpressed by his stupid behaviour, but do not forget to be nice to him when he does behave.

The right position for a dog to be able to protect his owner.

Dogs in public places must wear collars, and your dog should also wear one at home. This is especially important if you have a new dog, as it allows you to handle him or correct him, as in the situation just described, without 'grabbing' at him.

GUARDING A LITTER

A number of bitches dislike strangers looking at their pups, and are often very protective when the puppies are very young. This is natural, and they are instinctively guarding and protecting their pups. Not all bitches do this, and, as we have already said, in some of today's show-bred dogs, the instincts have been weakened. By the time pups are four or five weeks old, any bitch should allow anyone to look at her pups – in the presence of her owner.

Our first Australian Cattle Dog, Honey, was a keen guard. This breed is noted for its guarding instinct, but she loved to show off her pups to all and sundry so long as one of us was there. When they were tiny she would roll over on her side as if to say "Look what I've got, aren't they lovely!" However, we doubt if a stranger walking in on his own would have got a very friendly welcome. All her pups grew up to be first-class guards, but none were over-aggressive.

Some bitches like to show off their puppies, but others can be over-protective in the presence of strangers.

Photo: Keith Allison.

THE GOOD GUARD

Some people have misconceived ideas of what constitutes a good guard. If their new puppy does not bark at strangers by the time he is about four months old, they are disappointed, but a four month-old puppy who barks at strangers is almost invariably nervous or aggressive. If the former, he is barking because he is afraid and is trying to tell the stranger to go away. If the stranger does not go away, or approaches the puppy, it is pretty certain that he will run away. That sort of pup is likely to grow into a dog which whips round the back of a stranger, bites him on the leg, and then disappears! Unfortunately it is also the sort of dog which, if cornered, perhaps by a child wanting to make friends, is liable to bite quite viciously.

The aggressive puppy who stands his ground at four months will, almost certainly, become even more aggressive and, depending on his size, could become quite dangerous if the problem is not quickly dealt with. Be careful not to confuse aggression with dominance. A bold, extrovert puppy may well challenge his owner – or a visitor – but he is not necessarily being aggressive, only testing the water to see how far he can go. Obviously, he must be checked.

All pups should be friendly with everyone, although some breeds are more reserved than others, which makes it difficult, when looking at a litter, to know which will make good guards and which will not. The best guide lies in the pedigree – the dogs from which the puppy is descended – and this applies particularly to the dam. Not only do her puppies inherit her genes, but they are also influenced by her behaviour while they are in the nest. An aggressive bitch can be expected to have aggressive puppies, even if they have a friendly sire.

It is often thought that, if a dog is friendly towards strangers, it is no use as a guard, but this is by no means always the case. As we know, the dog's senses and reflexes are far more acute than our own. Instincts, particularly the guarding instinct, can be activated by stimuli too slight for us to notice. In the days when naughty children were given a good smack, some parents had to be careful to see that the family dog was not nearby as many would be likely to leap to the protection of the child. Judy, a Border Collie bitch who lived with us to a ripe old age, was a really soppy dog, friendly with everyone, but, if either of us pretended to attack the other, she would rush to protect the 'victim', getting very excited and barking and jumping up at the 'aggressor', clearly telling him to stop it. She never bit us, but we had no doubt at all that, if either of us had been attacked by a stranger, she would have bitten the attacker.

It is often difficult to assess what the reactions of a dog will be under unfamiliar circumstances, even if you know the dog quite well. Many people are sure that their dog is far too friendly to be of any help at all if they were to be attacked, but we believe that the majority of sensible dogs of all breeds will make some effort to protect their owner if they think the danger is real.

TRAINING FOR GUARDING

Most dogs have a sort of 'sixth sense' which makes them behave very differently when faced with real danger. When security officers first started using dogs, John trained quite a few to attack and sold them for that purpose. He was once offered a Boxer dog belonging to a couple who had a retail shop and lived in the flat above. If Buster heard someone coming into the shop, he would, if he got the chance, nip down stairs and stop them going any further, which was not very good for business!

In those days, we taught dogs to attack in play, which is now the general practice with police forces. First of all, the dog was encouraged to play with and hang on to a piece of sacking. Once he was enthusiastic about this, the sacking was wrapped around the 'criminal's' arm and the dog was spurred on to grab hold of it. In fact, the dog was responding to the hunting instinct rather than to the guarding instinct, but a criminal with 80lbs of dog locked onto his arm is not going to worry about instincts! For some reason, Buster did not want to play, and had no intention of worrying a piece of sacking. So John tried the old-fashioned method, where the dog is teased to make him angry in

Trained guard dogs need courage, but should always be under control.
Photo: Alan Jones.

the hope that he would then bite the arm of the teaser. No luck there either. Buster just did not want to know, but we had no reason to disbelieve his previous owners and felt sure that he would guard if we could only find something to trigger him off.

John decided to move to a realistic scenario. He enlisted the help of a friend, who often acted the part of a 'criminal', and was very experienced. Next to our property was an empty, rather dilapidated old shed with a lane running alongside it. The 'criminal' was dressed in a full padded suit which, in itself, makes someone look rather like a monster. As dusk approached, he went and hid in the shed, the dog not having seen him at all. He approached the shed through the field to avoid leaving a track along the lane. It was all to be a big surprise for Buster. John waited until it was almost dark, which is important, as a dog is much more alert to danger then than in daylight. He put Buster on a lead and casually walked along the lane towards the shed. As they approached, the criminal made a slight noise, not loud, but loud enough for Buster to hear. Buster stopped dead in his tracks, hackles raised, and started to growl. John praised and encouraged him with an excited "What is it then, who's there?", but, this time, Buster needed no encouragement and was straining at the lead. Next, John called to the criminal to come out, which he did, yelling and waving a stick in the air. Immediately, this dog, which previously had given the impression that he would not hurt a fly, changed into a completely different animal. He tore into the criminal and would certainly have badly injured him had he not been so well padded. From that minute on, Buster would attack anyone who threatened his handler, although he remained just as friendly towards people who did not present a threat. In fact, he then went out to Cyprus to act as guard to a family with children who were worried about their safety, as it was the time of the troubles there.

THE HUMAN ELEMENT

Like all other instincts, the guarding instinct can be encouraged or discouraged. This depends, firstly, on the strength of the instinct in the individual dog, and, secondly, on the personal circumstances and requirements of the owner. It is worth bearing in mind that the over-friendly dog with little or no guarding instinct may be of little help in time of need, but is not likely to get its owner into trouble either. On the other hand, if your dog bites someone who tries to steal your purse, you are liable to be sued for damages by the attacker! He may get off with a caution, but you could be liable for vast compensation and the dog could be sentenced to death.

It is quite common for dogs to resent other dogs approaching their owners, and some may attack or attempt to attack. Such dogs are really guarding their owners against strange dogs. Unwittingly, the majority of owners encourage such behaviour. They stroke their dog, and, in soothing tones, tell him not to worry, that the other dog is not going to hurt him, and a lot more rubbish besides. In fact, they are praising the dog and encouraging him to do what they do not want. In most cases, when a dog behaves like this, it is the fault of the owner.

Owners of puppies are usually far more scared that another dog will hurt their pup than the pup is himself, so the minute they see another dog they put the pup on a lead, or, if he is already on one, shorten it up. This is frequently followed by a lot of petting and soothing talk, telling the pup that he will be OK. Very often, the owner shouts at the other dog and shoos him away, however friendly he is. No wonder that, quite soon, the pup, who probably only wanted to have a game with the other dog, begins to perceive other dogs as threats. This problem could easily have been avoided if the advice given on socialising a puppy had been taken.

It is a sad fact that many dogs are accused of being vicious when, in fact, they are only responding to an instinct which makes them want to protect their owner. An animal really cannot help following an instinct and, while it is essential to control it and sometimes find another outlet for it, there is no point in trying to 'knock it out of him'. Primitive people still retain many of the instincts which have been lost to most so-called civilised people, but we are still attracted to members of the opposite sex – most of us, anyhow! Few people know exactly why they are attracted to a particular person, and even fewer ever know where this attraction will lead them – sometimes great happiness, sometimes tragedy. Whatever the outcome, it occurs in spite of the fact that we are able to reason and think about what we are doing. The poor dog, who cannot reason in the same way that we do, simply follows his instinct. Too many people think that he should know right from wrong without making any attempt to teach him.

It is important to remember that a dog's reaction to a human being is very different from his reaction to other dogs. Politicians appear to be unable to realise this fact, which has been proved by legislation which discriminates against 'fighting breeds', particularly Pit Bull Terriers. These breeds, however, have been bred to attack and, if possible, kill other dogs – not people. Otherwise, it would have been impossible to handle them during organised dog fights. The majority are, in fact, very trainable, friendly with children and adults, and seldom have much of a guarding instinct. The trouble arises because they just love to worry anything, and really enjoy being swung around while hanging onto a piece of rope or even a plank of wood. Of course, it is very easy to teach such a dog to attack anything, including people, on command. If they do attack, their enormously powerful jaws can cause quite horrific injuries.

A dog's reaction to children is often quite different from his reaction to adults. Some dogs adore children, but others definitely do not. Sometimes this attitude is not entirely the dog's fault. When asked if a certain dog or a certain breed is 'good with children', our usual reply is "Are the children good with dogs?"

CHAPTER SIX

MATCH MAKING

Choosing the right dog for your particular life style deserves considerably more thought than most people give to it. You are choosing a companion, hopefully for the next ten to fifteen years. If you get it wrong, neither of you will be very happy.

However much care you take, there are times when the wrong dog has been picked, or when your lifestyle changes so much that you can no longer give your dog the quality of life he deserves. If this should happen, do not, as so may owners do, struggle on for years. It may be very difficult for you to accept that your dog, brought up from a puppy, now gives you little pleasure, and could be far happier with a new owner. Often, a dog who seems to be a 'square peg in a round hole' develops into a completely new animal in a different home. If you do not suit each other, let the dog have another chance, and you will both be much happier.

THE WRONG REASONS

Before deciding on a dog, go along to see some breeders and to small shows, where you will see many different breeds, usually owned by people who will gladly tell you all about them. Go to Agility shows or Trials where you can see dogs working, and take your time – it is worth it. Read books on the breed, but with caution! Most, but not all, writers of breed books are ardent fans of their chosen breed, and extol its virtues but are blind to its faults.

Too many people choose their dog for the wrong reasons. They go along to a Dog Show, or see a dog on television, and like the breed. It is the right size, has a lovely shiny, long coat, it is just the right colour,

Make sure you learn as much as possible about the breed before buying a dog.

it really is beautiful and just what they want – but is it? They know nothing about the breed; it is not so much what the dog looks like, as what makes it 'tick', that matters.

Sometimes, owners who have recently lost their old friend rush out and buy a puppy of the same breed. They could be lucky and find a charming puppy, very similar in many ways to the dog they have lost, but dogs are individuals. If you have an empty breakfast cereal packet, and you buy another of the same brand, the contents will be identical. Although a pup of the same breed will be like the old dog in some ways, it will not be a replica of it. We have had people ring us up for help, saying that their new pup does this and that – things which old Rusty never did – what can they do? Poor little pup, he is only being himself – so take care.

An example of a bad choice was a neighbour who went to a Horse Show and arrived back with a boisterous Border Collie pup. Why? Because she had seen his father there and thought he was the best-behaved and most intelligent dog she had ever seen. Maybe he was, but the pup proved to be a disaster. He was not easy to train, he ran off, he was aggressive towards other dogs and he bit his owner. A little more thought and trouble in finding out more about the breed would have saved much heartbreak and unhappiness for both dog and owner.

RESCUED DOGS

If you take a dog from an Animal Rescue Centre, you are undoubtedly doing it a good turn. You could be lucky and find you have a really nice dog, but there can be difficulties. It is not always possible to find out much about the dog's background, although staff will be able to tell you how the dog behaves in kennels, with people and other dogs. Many homes now have resident behaviourists who will talk to you, explain any problems the dog has, and discuss with you whether or not they think the dog would be suitable.

Although there can be problems, many of these dogs end up as good companions, and, if there are unacceptable difficulties, then most organisations will take the dog back.

WORKING BREEDS

We have seen that, whilst all dogs have the same basic instincts, the strength of these can vary a great deal between breeds and individuals of each breed. In most so-called working breeds, man has, by selective breeding, strengthened the instincts which are of most use to him. This is most noticeable in gun dogs, where the Field Trial strains are very different from the Show strains. This is not to say that many show-bred dogs will not work – they may well do so – but very, very few will ever make Field Trial Champions. If you want a gun dog as a companion and pet dog, then buy one from a show strain. In many working Spaniels, such as Springer Spaniels, the working instinct is so strong that it overrides all else. Many of this breed work successfully as 'sniffer' dogs, detecting drugs or explosives. In fact, many are given from private homes where they were far too hyperactive and excitable, but, once trained to use their noses, these dogs have endless stamina and enthusiasm to work.

Most gun dogs are very trainable. They have been bred to work with man, and to work as he directs, for a very long time. Nearly all are natural retrievers, and one of the best ways to reward a Retriever or Spaniel is to allow him to retrieve something.

Most Spaniels and Retrievers have strong retrieving instincts; puppies of these breeds are likely to pick up anything and everything in sight, and usually they will bring it to you in triumph, with a wagging tail and a broad grin. This is often the time when dog and owner have a misunderstanding. The pup is doing what comes naturally, and he is also doing what he thinks will please his owner. After all, yesterday he brought his ball and his favourite toy and was praised for it. Today he brings a new

The English Springer Spaniel: A tireless worker with great stamina. Retrieving is a good outlet for his energy.

Photo: Steve Nash.

The Golden Retriever: A popular companion dog.

Photo: Carol Ann Johnson.

hat, carelessly thrown on a chair, or a rather special cream scarf which does not improve with slobber all over it! So, he is soundly cursed and the precious item grabbed out of his mouth, leaving one very upset and confused puppy. If you want him to retrieve happily then never scold him for bringing you anything – even a very dead rabbit! Prevention is always better than cure, and the easy way out is to pick things up and not leave them where the pup can find them. Be fair, he is only a baby trying his best.

Teach him to retrieve properly and you will have a lot of pleasure together. He can be taught to bring the paper, your slippers, his lead and so on. He can also be taught to find lost objects – start by throwing his ball into long grass and sending him to fetch it. On a country walk, drop his lead without him seeing, and send him back along your track to find it. To the dog, all of this will be a game where he can use his nose and his desire to retrieve; it gives him something to do – idle dogs are seldom happy ones. And he will be doing it for you, his leader, and not simply to amuse himself.

HOUNDS
Hounds fall into two groups; the sight hounds, such as Salukis and Greyhounds, and the scent hounds, such as Otterhounds and Bassets.

SIGHT HOUNDS
Sight hounds have excellent sight for any moving object, be it a rolling ball or a rabbit in the distance. They have been bred for centuries to hunt and kill their prey. In today's world, this can be a problem. If not controlled, it is not unknown for a sight hound to chase and kill a neighbour's cat or even a small dog, not because he is a vicious animal, but because his genes are programmed to make him want to chase. The result is that many of these hounds are never let off the lead because the owner is scared of what might happen. These hounds derive more enjoyment from just running free than from anything else, so the answer has to lie in training.

Even before training, the small puppy must be socialised with people, and, even more importantly, with other dogs of all shapes and sizes, if possible. Once used to small dogs, he is less likely to want to chase them, and, if he should by mistake chase, he is less likely to do any harm. Above all, these hounds must be taught to respond instantly to a recall, and also be taught to drop on command. A dog will often drop, if he has been taught to do so, more easily than he will do a recall. Once a hound is chasing something, it is useless calling and shouting, you will simply look stupid, and the dog will not even hear you. Once his mind is on the chase, he is deaf to all else. So, unless you are in some large open space with no game or livestock present, keep your hound on a lead if you cannot rely on him to come back. Even if you can rely on him to come back, keep him within sight. No dog out of sight can be said to be under control.

Apart from chasing a ball or racing around with a companion, there are other ways of providing an outlet for this hunting instinct. There is Whippet racing, Afghan racing (where other hounds are usually welcomed), lure coursing and other canine sports. Some owners are apt to think that if they let their dog go lure coursing or racing after a dummy hare, he will chase cats and small dogs. No, he will not, if he has been taught as a puppy to leave them alone. Most hounds are far

The Greyhound: Control is essential in a breed with such a strong hunting instinct.

Photo: Steve Nash.

from stupid – although some like to make you think they are – and soon learn the difference between going for a walk and going racing.

SCENT HOUNDS

Scent hounds are different inasmuch as the priority in their lives is scent. A scent hound will be at his happiest when following a scent, although in most, food comes a close second! Like a sight hound chasing prey, a scent hound with his nose on a scent trail is deaf to everything. Most have been bred to hunt in packs, and, when hunting, are under the control of the Huntsman. It is not unusual to see a number of different packs of hounds in the main ring at an Agricultural Show – Bassets, Beagles, Harriers, Foxhounds – each pack with its own Huntsman. These can all run loose together, but will immediately answer their own Huntsman's call, and separate into their own packs. A lone hound is not usually as willing to be obedient – he just does not see the point. The pack returns to the Huntsman because he supplies their pleasure – the hunt.

We once had a Bloodhound named Humperdink, and, at the time, we were living near a forest. We had a pack of about 20 mixed dogs, which were used for film work. They were exercised in the forest, about ten at a time, behind one of us on horseback. Humpy proved a problem. If he picked up a human scent, he would put his nose down, give tongue and was away, with the others following. We solved the problem by someone keeping Humpy at home when Mary went riding with the others. After half an hour or so, he would be let loose on the line Mary had taken. Down would go his nose and nothing would stop him until he caught up. Once he ran right through a group of hikers. As he was giving tongue, they scattered in all directions, obviously thinking the Hound of the Baskervilles was after them! Once he caught us up, he was then quite happy to stay, presumably because he had done his hunting for the day.

Another scent hound we had, who was a great character, was Bertie, a Basset hound. A lady living near us had to part with him when he was 18 months old. She had four children and another on the way, and had

The Basset Hound: Not an easy dog to train, but he can make an affectionate family dog. Don't let him hunt! Photo: Sally Anne Thompson.

decided that either a child or the dog must go, and thought it should be the dog! We went to see Bertie, as we were then always looking for dogs who could be trained for film work. When we first met Bertie, he was giving tongue in a very large garden, with his nose down on the trail of a pet rabbit, which had the run of the garden. He was so busy tracking, he ran right up to the rabbit (which was obviously used to it), sat down, wagged his tail and licked the rabbit's face. The family could not keep him, as, if he was taken for a walk, he just put his nose down on a scent and went off for hours. So, we bought him and he proved to be a very useful member of our team, but would still try to go hunting if he got the chance.

For anyone with a Bloodhound, there are Bloodhound Trials, where hounds hunt 'the clean boot'; or Bloodhound packs which hunt a 'runner' on foot over several miles of open country. Recently, Otter hounds have also been used for tracking lost persons, with considerable success. Some of the smaller hounds, like Beagles, have been used for drug detection. Many hounds are easy-going, friendly individuals, but not all are suitable as family pets. Because they have lived in packs for many generations, most hounds find it difficult to adapt to being an only dog, and an unhappy hound can raise his voice in a loud and lengthy protest – not often welcomed by near neighbours.

Unlike the sight hounds, who seem able to curl up into a very small space (even the larger ones such as Salukis seem to take up little room), hounds such as Otterhounds and Bloodhounds do take up a lot of space and do not seem to have the knack of folding themselves up neatly.

TOY DOGS

So-called 'toy' dogs often lead miserable lives because they are completely misunderstood and frustrated. We consider this to be one of the main reasons why so many small dogs are labelled snappy, lazy, greedy, yappy or even aggressive. Small they may be, but most are bright and intelligent, quick to learn, tough and active – if they are allowed to be. All they want is to be allowed to live like a dog.

We live near a town which has a large population of retired people. Many of them want dogs for company, and these are often small dogs. It saddens us to see Chihuahuas being carried around in shopping bags; Pugs and Pekes being pushed about in babies' prams; others with woolly coats on, even in warm weather, and being carried in their owners' arms. Toy dogs are dogs, not toys. We have owned several Toy dogs – a Pekingese, a Pug, Papillons, Cavaliers and a Chihuahua, and had a lot of fun with all of them. All have been treated in exactly the same way as our bigger dogs. They want to behave like dogs and, whatever their size, have the same instincts, although, in some of them, they have become weakened.

The Chihuahua we now have goes for long walks, swims and enjoys retrieving fir cones. She also enjoys searching for these in heather or long grass, and has impressed an Otter hound-owning friend with her scenting ability.

A Pekingese we bought from her breeder at 10 months because she had been returned as unmanageable was a little horror – she loved to chase horses. John had an old hunter, Duncan, and she would rush after him and hang on to his heels. Luckily, he was a placid old boy, but it was not a good idea and we quickly stopped it, but not that easily.

Several Toy breeds can now be seen competing in Agility Competitions, and very good they are at it too.

Like larger dogs, Toy dogs need exercise, but they can, luckily, take quite a lot in a small space. If taught to retrieve, they can have lots of

The Pug: Toy breeds are intelligent, tough and active – if they are allowed to be.

Photo: Carol Ann Johnson.

fun and exercise chasing a ball in a small garden, or even indoors. Many owners keep their small pets away from bigger dogs, but this can be a mistake. As pups they should be taken to a 'Puppy Play School' – but make sure it is a good one with a responsible, knowledgeable person in charge. Your pup needs to mix with other puppies and dogs, but in controlled circumstances. We have heard some worrying stories of Toy dogs chased or roughed up by large, boisterous breeds; so make some enquiries before taking your pup along. Allowed to live like dogs, small ones will lead much healthier, happier lives, and the extra exercise might well do their owners good too.

The Staffordshire Bull Terrier: Tough and tenacious, but, in the right hands, he is an excellent companion.

Photo: Keith Allison.

BULL BREEDS

Many of the 'Bull' breeds, such as Bostons, French Bulldogs, Staffordshire Terriers, Bull Terriers and Boxers, can make very good companion dogs, if you understand them and their characteristics. Some were originally bred for dog fighting or are descended from fighting dogs, and, even today, many have a tendency to enjoy a good 'scrap'. They were never bred to attack people, although, sadly, today we have some thugs who train them for this purpose.

Usually, these breeds are very good with children. They are tough, insensitive dogs with a high pain threshold, and they seem able and willing to stand any amount of pulling about by children without getting annoyed; in fact, they seem to enjoy it.

A friend of ours who runs a very well known zoo always has French Bulldogs to play with her orphan chimps, which are being hand-reared.

Most Bull breeds are, to say the least, tenacious, and, if they get a grip on anything – animate or inanimate – they do not let go easily. So, the danger is that, if one does bite, it is usually a severe bite. Puppies love playing, and tug of war games are popular, but, until the pup has been taught to let go on command, it is best not to let children play in this way with the puppy. The pup could become far too excited, and the game end up in tears. He must be taught to let go immediately when told to.

Guarding breeds have been dealt with comprehensively in the chapter on the Guarding Instinct, but it is worth mentioning again that, if you want a dog as a guard, then you must be careful in your choice and remember that good temperament is of paramount importance.

TERRIERS
Terriers were originally bred to go to ground after foxes and rabbits,

Terriers are energetic, often noisy dogs, and need a very active lifestyle.
Photo: Amanda Bulbeck.

and to catch rats. In the mid 1800s, competitions to see how many rats a Terrier could kill in a rat pit in a given time were common. The record was held by a famous dog called Billy, who killed 100 rats in a pit in seven-and-a-half minutes. Yorkshire Terriers in those days did not have the long coats of the show ones of today. A Yorkie of about 6lbs was recorded as killing 20 large rats in three minutes – quite a feat for such a small dog. So it can be seen that Terriers were gutsy, tenacious dogs, used to working on their own. This is not to say that they are unintelligent; most are quite bright, but they are seldom too keen on learning obedience. Mary did have a Wire Fox Terrier in the 1950s which she qualified Companion Dog; but we believe this is the only one of that breed to qualify in the UK.

Obviously, times have changed, and most of today's show-bred Terriers never see a rat and might be none too keen on tackling one if they did. Even so, many do retain some working instinct, and tend to be excitable little dogs, ready to find any excuse to bark or chase the neighbour's cat. Having no rats to kill, you can help them to get rid of their frustration by giving them 'tug toys' to play with and they will get a lot of pleasure from worrying these. Terriers also have a tendency to enjoy digging, not usually popular with gardeners. The best way to solve this problem for dog and owner is to build a small sand pit in the garden. It does not need to be very big; an odd, unused corner would be ideal. Block it in on three sides so that the sand does not scatter everywhere. Teach your dog to use it by burying toys or tidbits, and encouraging him to dig. Once he knows where he is allowed to dig, you can teach him that other areas in the garden are out of bounds. (Dachshunds also enjoy digging, and, if you have one, it will probably appreciate a sand pit too.)

Terriers need quite a lot of exercise to keep them fit and happy and, even if not ideal candidates for obedience competitions, must be taught to behave.

HERDING BREEDS
Herding breeds are usually amenable to training, as they have worked

with man for generations. Sheepdogs are often more submissive and responsive than Cattle dogs. Cattle are not so easy to move as sheep, and the Cattle dog must have initiative and courage to move them where they are wanted, and to avoid being kicked. Unless brought up properly, Cattle dogs as pets can cause problems, especially if there are noisy, extrovert children in the family. Most people have heard of one of the Queen's Corgis, which took a liking to nipping the Guardsmen on duty outside Buckingham Palace.

We once sold a delightful Corgi pup to a family who were very pleased with him, until one day we had a desperate phone call – he had bitten them all, and would we please take him back? He was only ten months old, and had a really nice temperament when we sold him, and

A cattle dog needs courage and determination.

Photo: Sally Anne Thompson.

so we were very puzzled. A little questioning revealed that, as a small pup, he had nipped their heels, which the kids thought very funny. So did the puppy, but, as he grew, he bit harder and ran faster. So, instead of teaching him not to do it, anyone wanting to leave the room waited until the dog was asleep and then rushed to the door, hoping to get out before he woke up. Needless to say, it did not work; he loved that game, and always beat them to the door. In fact, they made ideal cattle substitutes for him.

He came back to us, and, as it was near Christmas, we were giving displays at children's parties. The Corgi was quickly broken to harness, and took his place within a team of four Corgis pulling a miniature wagon. After a few weeks and some training, he was sold to a very nice French family, who were told about his previous problem. He lived in France for years, and travelled all over Europe, never biting or even nipping anyone again. He was not an aggressive dog, and had only bitten because his owners completely misunderstood him. If they had asked us about it when it first happened, they would not have had to part with him.

Most Herding breeds are very active, and need plenty of exercise and free running. They also need something to occupy their minds, and most are ideally suited for the many canine sports which have clubs in most areas.

HUSKIES

Huskies and the related Nordic breeds take to harness work like a duck to water. Although this cannot be called a natural instinct, it does seem to be an acquired instinct. If you have ever seen Husky racing, you will know how much enjoyment the dogs get out of it. Once they arrive at a race meeting, nothing will stop their excited barking. They simply love their work. These dogs, and some other Spitz breeds, have been bred to pull sleds and are tough, active dogs. They can withstand harsh Arctic conditions, and teams can pull a sled for many miles over the ice, day after day.

When we were actively involved in film work, we had a Husky called Pilot. He was not an easy dog to train, as we soon found out, but he lived outside and happily exercised with the other dogs. One day, we had an exceptionally heavy snow fall, and John phoned the editor of a children's television programme, asking if they would like to come and film a Husky pulling a sled. This was many years before Husky racing became known in the UK. They were keen to come down, and wanted to come that afternoon. As, at that time, we did not even have a sled for Pilot to pull, John persuaded them to come the next morning, and

The Siberian Husky: A workaholic who does not adapt easily to domestic life.

stayed up half the night making a sled. We already had a proper harness, and, as soon as it was light, we put Pilot in the sled. He had never been harnessed up before, but no sooner had we got him in than he was off, and we could hardly keep up with him. When the film cameraman arrived, he sat on the sled behind a small girl to film – quite a weight, but Pilot would happily have run on to the local village had we not stopped him. An example of an 'acquired instinct', or characteristic which has been added to a breed through breeding.

It is impossible to give such a dog enough exercise in a pet home; nor is it easy to teach him to walk quietly on a lead without pulling. So, the Husky is not really a suitable candidate for a soft life as a pet dog.

CROSSBREEDS AND MONGRELS

There are many people who prefer a crossbreed or a mongrel to a pure breed. As far as mongrels are concerned, we have known and owned some very good ones, but a mongrel puppy is often a bad bet. Their genetic make-up can be so varied and mixed that it is difficult, if not impossible, to say how the adult will turn out, mentally or physically.

Crossbred pups – that is, pups with two pedigree parents of different breeds – are more predictable. Golden Retriever/Labrador Retriever crosses are more successful as guide dogs than any other breed. We have heard it said that crossbred dogs will show the breed characteristics of the parent which it most resembles. Thinking back over the many crossbreeds we have owned and trained, we feel that this is often correct, but would not like to say that it is always so.

BREED-SPECIFIC BEHAVIOUR

So, it can be seen that there are many matters to be considered before you choose your dog. Although we have gone into some detail concerning the type of behaviour you might expect from your chosen breed, it must be emphasised that it only applies to the breed in general. Each dog is an individual. There are Newfoundlands who hate the sight of water, gun dogs with no interest in retrieving, hounds who would rather play with a rabbit than catch and kill it. There are also Corgis and Border Collies who work well to the gun, Pekingese who will kill mice as eagerly, though perhaps not so easily, as a terrier kills a rat, and Boxers who would love to go to sleep on your lap. Even so, behaviour which is specific to a breed is more usual.

Many years ago, when most dogs worked for their living, those that were no good at the job were simply shot. The only ones which were bred from were the good workers, and, as has been said, like begets like.

Once the Dog Show scene started to become more popular, good-looking dogs with little interest in work were sold to those wanting them for the show ring. This is an obvious reason why many dogs from show strains have much weaker instincts than their ancestors or their

Although these mongrel pups look alike now, they will probably all grow up differently.

working contemporaries.

In some ways, this can be an advantage to the pet owner, who has no desire for his dog to kill rats or work sheep. This is not to say that the dog will not want to do these things; you must always bear in mind the purpose for which the dog was originally bred.

NEUTERING

If you do not want to breed from your dog, then we strongly advise neutering. Male dogs tend to have some anti-social habits. Often, they will lift their legs in the most unwelcome places; they will mount legs, children and the family cat, if allowed. Should there be a bitch in season in the vicinity, then your entire dog will probably keep everyone awake all night, howling; if he can escape, he will be off down the road trying to find her. Not all dogs have a very strong sex drive, but, if they do and they have no outlet for their desires, then life can be very frustrating for them and make you very unpopular with your neighbours.

In the case of bitches, their whole life is geared to reproduction. With a few breed exceptions, most bitches come into season twice a year for approximately three weeks. If mated, a bitch will produce pups nine weeks later. If not mated, many bitches still think that they are going to produce pups nine weeks later! This is known as a pseudo or phantom pregnancy. Such bitches behave exactly as if they were in whelp. At about nine weeks, they produce milk, become very broody, dig up their beds and carry toys, socks or slippers there and guard them as they would a real litter. The bitch is not being awkward, she cannot help it; she is behaving as her hormones tell her she should. She may need veterinary treatment, and this type of behaviour causes a lot of disruption in the family.

When they are in season, bitches need to be kept under strict supervision and not allowed near any male dogs – and, believe us, some are very cunning about finding a lover down the road! If you have a bitch in season and a male dog in the same household, then that is a recipe for disaster, even a nervous breakdown – yours!

We consider it much kinder to have a dog/bitch neutered. An excellent small-animal vet we knew kept records of all the bitches she had spayed, and found that they needed to visit her far less frequently than those bitches who had not been spayed.

For many years we have made a point of having any dog we did not need for breeding neutered. Neutering does not change a dog's personality. It eliminates much unwanted behaviour – behaviour which is natural to the dog but which can cause him a lot of frustration if he is checked for indulging in it. One advantage is that neutered animals are often more affectionate and more closely bonded to their owners.

Until comparatively recently, there was widespread prejudice against neutering either dogs or bitches, and few vets would carry out the operation. Neutering of either sex was claimed to result in obesity and lack of character, and this certainly has happened. But it is not neutering that causes the problem, it is neutering when the animal is too young. We have seen dogs which were castrated at four or five months of age which grew up to be fat 'eunuchs'. This does not happen if the animal is allowed to mature before the operation. It is worth remembering that the chief cause of obesity in dogs, as in humans, is too much food and too little exercise.

Guide dogs for the blind are all neutered, as are most assistance dogs today. The Guide Dogs for the Blind Association's policy in the UK is to wait until the male is about eight months of age. Bitches are neutered after their first season. However, neutering is not a cure for all evils. We have met owners who have had their dogs castrated in the hope that it would "cure" them of fighting – but it hasn't worked! This has often been advised by a vet, who should have know better.

Sex is usually the catalyst which triggers aggression between males of all species! So it is obvious that removing the sex drive should, at the same time, remove the desire to fight. This usually happens; but not if the dog has already become an habitual fighter who fights because he enjoys it. Nor will it cure the nervous dog who fights because he is afraid of being attacked and tries to get one in first.

GENETIC DEFECTS
In some breeds, unfortunately in too many, there are genetic health defects. These include hip dysplasia, elbow dysplasia, eye problems such as progressive retinal atrophy and Collie eye anomaly, deafness, digestive problems and many more. Reliable, honest breeders will have their stock tested for hereditary diseases common to their breed, and will usually be happy to discuss any problems with you.

YOUR LIFESTYLE
Then there is your own behaviour to consider. Are you a strong-minded person who demands instant obedience, or a laid-back one who takes life as it comes? Do you enjoy walking and outside activities, or are you a couch potato? Are you young or old? Do you like a neat, tidy house and a manicured lawn? If so, maybe you should forget about having a dog. Are you out a lot, do you have children, or are you going to have a baby? Does your partner like dogs, or just tolerate them? If you live with anyone else or have a family, it is important that the whole family want a dog. If someone in the household dislikes the dog, then sooner or later the dog will become distressed and confused. All these things, and many more, need to be considered before you decide to have a dog. With care over choosing the right dog, understanding and training, you should be able to enjoy a happy relationship for many years. Never forget that he is a dog, and however much you train him and however long he lives with you, he will still think like a dog and behave like a dog.

CHAPTER SEVEN

SOCIAL BEHAVIOUR AND EARLY TRAINING

However much trouble and care you have taken to find out all you can about your new puppy, he will have had no chance at all to find out anything about you – his new pack leader. He will have come straight from his family pack, where he was disciplined and loved by his dam, and had fun and games and learned the beginnings of canine behaviour from his siblings. The move to a new home is a traumatic experience.

DISCIPLINE AND LOVE

Many researchers consider that one reason man domesticated the wolf was that the structure of the wolf pack was very similar to that of the human family group. This may well have been so at that time, when both wolf and man hunted for their food and guarded their territory against predators or enemies, but the family of today is completely different. Family life can and often is chaotic and unstable, nearly always noisy with people coming and going, making it difficult for the pup to know who actually belongs to his pack.

Discipline in your puppy's canine pack was easy to understand. Discipline in the human group can be lax and erratic. We humans are a devious lot; we say one thing and mean another. We tell lies, and are inconsistent when enforcing a rule. The dog is an honest animal with no such trickery, and can find us very difficult to understand. But, for all that, in time, many wise old dogs have their humans summed up pretty well!

It is well-known that human babies deprived of affection and physical contact can not only become very withdrawn, but may even die. Your puppy is the same; his mother corrected him firmly and quickly, but, once he behaved, she would soon be affectionate again and would never bear a grudge. As the pup grows older he would, had he been left with a canine pack, have started to learn from the older dogs. These would have taken over from his dam as far as discipline was concerned; in other words, he was learning the rules of the pack and his place in the hierarchy. He has to do exactly the same in this new pack of humans. He has to learn respect and that his place is at the bottom of the pack, but do not shout and bully; always be fair and give him plenty of affection as well as training.

Children and dogs can be great friends, but small children must not be left alone with any dog.   *Photo: Sally Anne Thompson.*

Some of your rules will seem very odd, even stupid to him. Why can he dig in the sand pit and not the garden? Why can he chew up his own toy but not a lovely pillow full of feathers? It just does not make sense to a canine mind. You will have to make him understand that, stupid as they may seem, your rules have to be obeyed.

Make sure that, when he is a small puppy, you never allow him to do anything that he will be prohibited from doing when he is older. For example, your lovely Golden Retriever snoozing on your lap will not be so welcome when he is grown up.

The new puppy is going to have a lot to learn in a short time, and will need a great deal of understanding from you. He does not know what you consider right or wrong, and it is your job to teach him; but he is still a baby and he needs lots of love and affection.

TRAINING BASICS

A small puppy needs to learn the basics of training, but his attention span will be very short, so keep the lessons short and keep them fun. Training should be a game to the dog, but a game where you are always in charge. Never try to train if you are feeling off-colour, tired, or worse, in a bad temper; you will do more harm than good. Never train your pup/dog if he is unwell, tired, full of dinner or over-excited. A dog

First lessons on a lead – never pull the pup.

Photo: Sally Anne Thompson.

which has just been given some exercise will concentrate far better than one which is itching to go for a run.

When teaching something new, use both verbal and physical praise and make sure your timing is right – praise as he does what you want, not seconds after. Here, again, you must get to know your dog. Some laid-back types need stimulating with a large amount of vocal praise, patting and hugging. A more sensitive type may jump out of his skin if you give him a hefty pat on the rump, and may think he is being punished; so find out what is the best praise for your own dog.

He needs to learn his name and the meaning of the word "No". Try to pick a suitable name. We were once given a very tough Border Collie called Pansy, and a Golden Retriever called Woof! Pick a short name; make sure everyone uses the same name to call him, and never use his name if you have to scold him.

TEACHING HIM HIS NAME
The easiest way to teach him his name is with the use of treats. Call him in an encouraging tone, and, when he runs to you (as most pups will), give him a treat and a hug and praise him well. Do not make the mistake of calling him when he is sniffing around the dustbin, watching a bird on the lawn or some other distraction. Wait until he is looking your way and you are far more likely to get the result you want. Never keep on calling and calling; in no time at all the pup will regard your voice as just another noise, like the radio. Praise him every time he comes, but gradually cut down on the treats and just give them occasionally.

TEACHING "NO"
Unfortunately, your pup also needs to learn "No" and what it means – "Stop doing that at once", or, if you see him about to do something wrong and catch him in time, "Don't do it".

As with small children, life for a young puppy can seem to be made up of an awful lot of No's, which can make them quite depressed if you are not careful. So, when you teach the meaning of "No", decide upon

Teaching a puppy to sit.
Photo: Sally Anne Thompson.

a word which means "Yes, you can". This is what is termed a 'release' word and we usually use "OK", but any word or short phrase will do, as long as you always use the same one. It might mean "OK, you can dig in your sand pit/chew your toy/have a bark", and so on. We all work better for a reward, so never forget the praise – a happy dog learns faster.

TEACHING "COME" AND "SIT"

A pup can easily be taught to come and to sit at the same time. Call him to you in a happy, encouraging tone. When he arrives in front of you, hold your hand, with a treat in it, over his head, at the same time saying "Sit". As he looks up at your hand, move it further back over his head; as his eyes follow your hand he should (and most will) sit automatically. If he does, immediately give him the treat and praise him well – but not too enthusiastically, as it will only get him excited. If he does not sit properly, use your other hand to push his quarters down gently and reward him as before. Keep him there a few seconds before releasing him with an "OK". Repeat this a few times, but not too often as he will only become fed up.

Once he knows what you want and is responding, only reward him with food at random. You do not want him to start thinking of you as a mobile food-dispenser. Once he is sitting promptly on command, practise in different places. A dog taught to sit in the kitchen only can become confused and refuse to sit outside or in another room. Try to teach this exercise in as many different places as possible, and keep him sitting for a little longer each time.

You can call him for his dinner, have him sit and stay, place his dinner on the floor but make him wait until you say "OK" before he eats it. He should have already learned "No" and, if he looks like moving, growl "No" at him.

TEACHING "DOWN"

One of the easiest ways to teach the "Down" is from the "Sit". Tell your dog to sit, using both vocal and hand commands. Once he is sitting, lower your hand with a food treat in it down to the ground, just in front of his nose, saying "Down". If he goes straight down, give him the treat and praise him. If he tries to wriggle forward, hold him back with your other hand, pressing on his shoulders. As with the Sit, keep practising this until he will go down on command to either a hand or vocal signal. Increase the time you make him stay down, but do not expect too much too soon.

Once he is steady, you can start leaving him and going out of his sight, making sure that you can still see him. If he moves, go back to him immediately, correct him and put him back in place. Leave him for a very short while, and go back and praise him.

Teaching the Down.   *Photo: Sally Anne Thompson.*

Staying down out of sight and dropping on command are both very important exercises and both can be life-savers. Many years ago, we had a Boston Terrier who was one of Mary's favourites, although we try not to have favourites! One very hot sunny day both of us took the day off and took Bossy with us. After a swim we left the beach and went to a café for a drink. Mary put Bossy down under the table; and when we finished our drink and left, we crossed the main road back to our car. Mary suddenly realised she had left Bossy in the café. She rushed into the cafe to the table where we had been sitting, which was, by then, occupied by another couple. Diving underneath she found Bossy exactly where she had been left, grabbed her up, and left a very bewildered couple staring after her! If Bossy had not been reliable on the Down, she would probably have been run over.

To start teaching the emergency Down, have your dog walking near you and suddenly tell him to "Down" in an urgent voice. If he does not obey immediately, push him down on his shoulders. When he goes down, make a great fuss of him and let him run off and play. Do this in all sorts of different places, on a walk, in the house, in the garden, anywhere. Make a game of it, try to catch the dog out when he is least expecting it and always praise him very well afterwards.

HOUSE TRAINING

Properly brought up puppies, by which we mean pups who have been reared in a clean environment with the opportunity to move away from their sleeping area to relieve themselves, are usually easy to house train. You should start to house train your puppy as soon as you have him home. The best and easiest way is to use a dog crate (also called a folding kennel or a travelling crate). Many people still throw up their hands in horror at the suggestion that they should put their dog in a crate, but a crate with newspaper on the floor, a comfortable bed and a toy to play with will soon become a den to the puppy – a place he can call his own, where he can be put if you are busy, and where the kids cannot pester him.

Introduce him to it by feeding him in it or putting a chew toy there.

Leave the door open to begin with. If you want him to go in, tell him "Bed", "In your house" or anything you like, but be consistent. Shut him in for a short while, and stay near him. Do not let him out if he is whining or scratching. Once he is quiet, tell him he is a good boy, and then let him out.

Soon, he should get used to spending time there when you are too busy to keep an eye on him. Take him out whenever he wakes up and after every meal, decide on a spot in the garden you want him to use and take him there. Teach him a word or short phrase such as "Hurry up", and immediately he performs, make a great fuss of him. Do not rush back inside; let him have a bit of a game and a sniff around first. Once you get to know your pup, you will recognise the signs which mean that he is in a hurry to go out – restlessness, turning round, sniffing or whining – and do not keep him waiting!

SLEEPING

Where you decide to let your dog sleep is up to you. The kitchen or utility room is often chosen, but if you want him to sleep in your bedroom, there is a lot to be said for that. He will have company, and, as a pack animal, no puppy relishes being alone. It establishes a firm relationship between you, and it makes for a quieter night, to start with. If you want, you can then gradually move the crate just outside your bedroom door, and finally, into whichever room you want. Few small puppies can last the night, and it is probably worth getting up to let him out. If you do not wake up in time and he has to go on the paper, never scold him, just take him out as soon as you can.

Apart from its use in house training and in teaching a pup to be left alone, a crate is useful in stopping bad habits from forming. In a crate, a puppy, or a dog, cannot chew the carpet, steal the dinner, chase the cat or do anything else you would prefer him not to do. If he never gets the chance to do these things, he is less likely to want to do them. A crate can also be used when travelling or when away from home. Most dogs will settle happily in strange places such as hotel rooms if they have their own den with them; and many hotels will allow a dog in a

A crate will keep a puppy out of mischief, as well as helping with house training and providing a safe 'den'.

Photo: Amanda Bulbeck.

room if he has his own crate, where they would not allow it if he was left loose when the owner was out.

WALKING ON A LEAD

A pup should be familiarised with on a lead as soon as you have him home. A puppy, like a toddler, has a lot to learn and a limited attention span, so a lead is a must if you take him out. Put a soft leather or nylon collar on him and leave it on for a few days. Take it off at night, as it might get caught on something. Keep encouraging the pup to follow you around, and make a great fuss of him when he does. Nearly all small pups want to follow someone, as they can quickly become lost. Once he is following you well and not bothering with the collar, put a light lead on. As before, encourage him to follow you, talk to him, and use tidbits if it helps. Many pups will trot along happily straightaway. Others go on strike and sit down; if this happens, just stand still (or squat down) and call him to you, not forgetting the praise. Some

A puppy should be accustomed to a collar and lead before attempting to get him to walk with you.

Photo: Carol Ann Johnson.

puppies object to the lead and throw themselves around. In this case, you should again stand still and let him fight himself to a standstill. Then, call him to you, and make a great fuss of him and start walking again. Just go a few steps and give him a tidbit; do not go on for too long, there is always tomorrow – but always end on a good note.

Some pups start to pull on the lead, which is a bad habit that should be nipped in the bud. Never pull against a dog – that is just what he wants. Try standing still until he stops, turn around quickly and walk in the opposite direction, where he will have to come too, or give a sharp tug on the lead giving the command "Heel", or whatever word you are using, and do not forget to reward when he responds.

RETRIEVING

Most dogs, even the Toy breeds, have a retrieving instinct. It may not be as strong as it is in a Retriever or a Spaniel, but the odds are that it is there, waiting to come out. If you have read the chapters on working dogs, you will realise how very important the retrieving instinct is in the work of these dogs, and how it can be diverted into many different channels to help in various ways.

You may only have a pet dog, but if you teach him to retrieve, his life will be much fuller, and you can have endless fun together. Many pet dogs develop problems because of boredom and too little exercise. There are all sorts of games you can play together, such as catching a Frisbee, retrieving a ball, looking for hidden articles in long grass, retrieving over jumps or scent discrimination. Scent discrimination is an excellent 'party piece', in which your dog finds a certain article from among several others – it always impresses non-doggy visitors!

You may not need an Assistance dog, but a dog who retrieves can make himself useful in the house. Fetching the mail, bringing your slippers, picking up his lead – all these things make him feel useful and a part of the family.

If you start early enough, most puppies will play with a ball or soft toy. Retrieving is part of the hunting instinct and, like all instincts, it can be strengthened by use and weakened, or even die, if not used. A puppy who shows signs of wanting to run after an object and pick it up should be encouraged and praised, even if he is bringing something you would rather not have. If a pup picks up something and brings it to you and you ignore him, it may well put him off the whole idea. It is even worse if he is scolded for picking something up and bringing it to you. He could pick up something you do not want him to have and rush around with it, refusing to give it up. The worst thing you can do is to shout at him and/or chase him.

So start by playing with the pup with a toy, or roll a ball along the ground. Make it exciting – do not just throw it and say nothing. Let the pup know how clever he is, and how pleased you are when he rushes after it and brings it back. Never pull, or try to pull, anything out of his mouth. If he is reluctant to give it up, offer a treat in exchange. This invariably works, but if it does not, then very gently press his top lips over his teeth, telling him to "Leave". When his mouth is open, remove the article very gently.

Once he has got the idea, you can start teaching him to sit and wait until you tell him to retrieve, and then to bring the article back and hold it in his mouth until you say "Drop it". Do not be in too much of a hurry; make sure he is really keen on retrieving first. Too much insistence on formal obedience in the early stages will only put a dog

This pup is enjoying a 'play retrieve' which forms the basis for the formal exercise to be taught later on.

Photos: Sally Anne Thompson.

off. Always throw the ball (or whatever article you are using) away from home. His instinct will make him want to bring it back – not necessarily to you, but if he is coming in your direction then you can probably intercept him. If he is the sort who runs around in circles, either run away from him – again, towards home – or simply sit down and wait. Sooner or later, most dogs, especially puppies, will come to investigate you. Above all, keep it fun. Some dogs are slow learners, some fast, so work out what suits your dog best. The more you train him, the more you will learn from him, and the better the understanding you will have between you.

SOCIALISATION

Socialisation is very important. If you have bought your pup from a responsible breeder, then he should have had a taste of it already. The dictionary defines 'socialise' as 'to fit for companionship with others; train or bring up so as to be well adapted, as in attitude and manners for life in society'. This sounds just what we want of our dogs, but it is not what is always given to them. Socialisation does not mean just trotting along to a puppy class a couple of times, or taking the pup out in the car and leaving it there while you go shopping. It means taking him to mix with children, other dogs and other animals if possible. Go to railway stations, shops, on buses, to schools, walk about in town and country, and go to puppy socialisation classes too. However, before you do, make very sure they are run by capable staff.

A single pup in a household has little chance of mixing with other canines, yet he must learn how to behave in canine company. He must learn how to play with other pups and older dogs, all of which is a lot of learning for a young pup. How much and how well he learns will depend a great deal on the structure of the class he attends. There should be a happy, confident atmosphere with knowledgeable people in charge.

Puppy classes should always have a few well-behaved, good-tempered adult dogs in attendance. It is far better for your pup to learn how to treat an adult dog under supervision than to make the wrong approach to a 'bully' dog in the park. Socialisation classes also give a pup the chance to mix with strangers, adults and children, and sometimes toddlers and babies – all of which will stand him in good stead later in life.

Whatever you do, try to avoid badly run puppy classes. A bad fright early on can have a disastrous effect on a puppy – often, a lasting one too. A Chihuahua pushed over and trodden on by a hefty and boisterous Retriever puppy may be terrified of large dogs all its life.

THINKING AND REASONING

Until recently, it was always said that dogs could neither think nor reason. But times have changed and now many people with dogs or who work with dogs will tell you they are quite sure that their dogs are capable of reasoning, although not in the same way that we do. Although dogs use vocal and body language, they have no words as such, only sounds. A dog will learn to sit just as easily if you use the command "stand" as if you use the the word "sit". Our language gives us not only the advantage of holding long conversations and discussions, but also of reading the written word, and that is what really makes us different from all other animals.

Cats and dogs can become friends...

...so can gundogs and rabbits.

Photo: Sally Anne Thompson.

Although it is generally agreed that dogs can think and reason – some more than others – unlike us, they do not worry about the bills being paid, about the havoc they created yesterday, or if they will have a run by the sea tomorrow. A dog lives for the moment. He does not think about the consequences of his actions. Neither does he do things out of spite. A pup may chew your slippers, pee on the carpet when you are out, bark and tear up a cushion. He does these things because he is bored, he wants some fun, he is lonely, he needed a pee and there was no-one to let him out. If you come back and punish him, he will have no idea what it is for – he cannot make the link between the punishment and his earlier 'crimes'.

BAD HABITS

Bad habits are not always easy to cure, so the best way is never to let them develop. Most so-called puppy crimes are the fault of the owner. Do not put temptation in his way. A dog cannot steal the Sunday roast if it is out of reach, eat the cat's dinner if it is picked up, pee in the bedroom if he is not in the bedroom, or chew your shoes if you put them away.

As we said earlier, it is your job to teach him right from wrong. Once he gets the idea, do not forget to praise him when he is doing right. All too often, owners scold a dog for doing wrong and then, when he does the right thing, never bother to praise him. Once he is house trained, it does not mean you should never praise him when he asks to go out or goes to the correct spot in the garden.

FUN

Your dog is, or certainly should be, a member of your family, but he is still a dog, and not a furry human. Dogs are very adaptable creatures and usually fit into our lives very well, and many appear to do their very best to do so.

In return, it is only fair that we allow them to behave as dogs, and, when possible, allow them to indulge in some natural fun. We believe that every dog has a right to run free, but he cannot do that safely unless

Every dog should be allowed to have fun, and this will help you build up a good relationship.

Photo: Keith Allison.

you have taught him to behave. He also needs to run and jump, roll in the grass – or mud – dig in the sand, chase a ball, sniff around where other animals have been, chew on his toys and play with other dogs. He also needs to bark. No-one wants a noisy dog, but most owners want a dog to bark a warning when someone calls at the house. They also want him to stop when told. The easiest way to stop a dog barking is to teach him to bark and to stop on command. Small children love to yell and shout when they are playing and rushing around letting off steam. Your dog is the same. If he is playing with another dog, let him bark if he wants, and if he barks with pleasure when he greets you, that is fine, as long as he stops when you say so. Or, maybe, on a country walk, let him have a barking session. To insist on silence except when he barks a warning is really rather unfair.

BENEFITS OF TRAINING

As we have said, in today's society a dog must be trained in basic obedience. A trained dog can safely be taken out and about. He will have more freedom than an untrained one; he will be a happier dog with a happier owner. A trained dog has a better relationship with his owner and there is a better understanding between them. Basic training is not very difficult. All dogs should come when called, walk quietly on a lead, sit and lie down and stay when told. You should be able to leave them alone in the house and, very importantly, tell them to drop instantly whenever and wherever told. This can be a life-saver – wherever you live, vehicles can suddenly appear, and if you can drop your dog, you should be able to prevent him from being run over.

CHAPTER EIGHT

WHEN THINGS GO WRONG

However carefully you bring up a puppy, there are bound to be times when things go wrong – and you wonder what on earth made you decide to have a dog in the first place! Do not despair – no-one, canine or human, is perfect. Problems can occur at any time, and although it may be difficult to find out the root cause, there is always a reason.

ADOLESCENCE

It does not take a detective to discover that adolescence is often the cause of problems. Your pup may have been behaving really well at training class and at home, but suddenly that can change. Your little angel becomes a tyrant.

The onset of adolescence varies between individuals and breeds. In Toy breeds, it is usually as early as five or six months; in small breeds, a little later; in large breeds around 10 – 12 months; but giant breeds can be as old as two or three years before they are fully mature.

Small puppies are usually fairly easy to train, with only the extra-dominant seeking a challenge at that age. Small pups need a leader, a

Swimming is excellent exercise for all dogs.

surrogate mother, someone to play with them, feed them, protect them and comfort them. Adolescence changes all that. In males, it usually occurs at about the time they first lift their legs. Life takes on a whole new dimension. There are interesting scents out in the park, attractive females which he never noticed before, or, if he did, they were just playmates. He feels the urge to mark his territory; he may even forget his house training. Some dogs become a little too enthusiastic about guarding the car, the house or their owner. The dog often becomes more independent and dominant, disobeying your commands, refusing to come when called, and so on.

Bitches usually change at about the time they have their first season. They are supposed to stay in season for three weeks – many have not read about that! Three weeks may be the norm, but some bitches go off after a couple of weeks, whereas others can stay on for five or even six weeks, during which time they must be kept away from male dogs. This is one reason, apart from their hormones playing up, that they tend to become moody, temperamental, nervous and inattentive. A bitch who has been used to going out for daily walks and free runs with your friend's male dog is now kept away from him, taken out on a lead and allowed little if any freedom. No wonder she is fed up!

Just for a minute let us compare adolescent dogs with adolescent children. In some ways (luckily, not all) they are very similar. Like dogs who forget their training, youngsters of this age can start doing badly at school; they no longer want to be with you on family holidays; they want their independence. Anyone who has had teenagers in the family knows only too well what is par for the course. Not all children turn into horrors during adolescence, and neither do all dogs. However, most teenagers and young dogs can display some very undesirable behaviour; but in the end, most turn out to be decent citizens or family companions.

WHAT TO DO

So, what to do about it? First and foremost, always remember that you are the boss, the pack leader, which does not mean that you cannot also be your dog's best friend. By fulfilling your role as pack leader, you will be ensuring that your dog has a happy life. He not only needs a pack leader, he wants one. If you let him take charge, he will only get into trouble and take you with him.

With dogs or bitches, the last thing you want to do at this stage in their lives is to shout and bully. That sort of behaviour will quickly make matters worse.

BITCHES

If you have a bitch, she is less likely to challenge you than a dog; in fact, a number of bitches, when they reach their first season, become nervous and upset about life in general. Obviously, this needs careful and sympathetic handling – but not too much sympathy. If she is suddenly frightened of, say, traffic, you will do no good standing at the roadside, patting her and telling her that it is OK, and that you will look after her every time she flinches at a passing car. Have her sitting beside you, and when a car approaches, talk to her in a cheerful tone of voice, and if she stays sitting, give her a treat and then praise her. Walk her about near traffic, try to distract her with a treat or a toy – do not throw it, just let her play with it in your hand. End up by giving her a free run somewhere safe. Try to make life interesting and do not shut her away on her own more than you have to. Do not attempt too much training, either. She will have a very short attention span at this time, and you will do better just concentrating on play training for the time being.

DOGS

Your dominant, independent fellow is a different matter. He is feeling his feet and not trying very hard to remember all the training he has already had. You have to gain his attention, give him some interesting things to do, take him to different places, keep him guessing. Make sure he does what he is told, when he is told. A dog lying down on the third command is not obedient. Take him out on the lead and do some heel work; it concentrates the mind. If he does not keep up with you, he gets a jerk; if he does, he gets praised. If he lags, you turn around sharply in a different direction and he will soon find it easier to follow you. If you wish, give him the odd food reward, but not too many. People who dish out treats for everything the dog does end up with a dog who loves his food and not his owner.

If you have had the dog since he was a puppy, you should understand each other's body and verbal language. If he needs correcting, a look may be sufficient to make him think again, or a harsh, growled "No", and, if he is still disobeying, a sharp jerk on the lead. Never forget to praise him when he does respond.

A good exercise for any dog who forgets how he should be behaving is the long Down. For one thing, it puts him in a submissive position. You can read the paper, watch the television or listen to the radio, but do make it a long Down, not just a few minutes. Any dog should be able to stay lying down for half an hour or more. Reward him with a game afterwards.

CANINE RELATIONS

During this growing-up period, dogs who have consistently appeared friendly towards other dogs can decide to challenge them and to be aggressive. A number of dogs are worse on the lead than off. In many cases, it is the fault of the owner. The dog lunges at the end of the lead and either barks or growls. So the owner tugs on the lead, shouts and tries to run away with the dog, which simply encourages the dog to have a go. As far as he is concerned, you dislike the other dog as much as he does. Here, you will need the help of some friends who own friendly dogs. Take your dog out for a walk on a lead and ask your friend to walk her dog past, on a lead, at a reasonable distance. If your dog starts to rant and roar, make him sit and tell him to be quiet. Immediately, get your friend and the dog to walk back again. Soon your dog should be sitting quietly, and, once he is, praise him well. Do the same thing again and again with different dogs if possible, until your dog gets the message that if he goes wild, he just gets ignored; but if he behaves, he gets rewarded.

For dogs who have a tendency to fight or chase when running free, you need different tactics. Our local dog wardens say they have more complaints about dogs chasing other dogs – usually small ones – than any other dog problems. Although some owners seem to think that it is funny when their great big lout chases a small dog, it is most definitely not. We know this only too well. Recently, Mary was walking in the forest with our Chihuahua and our Nova Scotia Duck Tolling Retriever. A lady appeared with two Rottweilers, which both appeared friendly. Our two dogs decided that discretion was the better part of valour, and took avoiding action by doing a detour through the woods. One Rottweiler immediately followed them, and cornered the Chihuahua under a bush and started barking and scrabbling at it. Mary asked her owner to call her dog off, but was told that the dog always went hunting in the forest, and that she was just hunting our dog but that she would not hurt him. She then walked away. Mary immediately went to the rescue, and it needed quite a few words in her best ex-Army Sergeant manner before the dog went away. Still, the owner never called it. This is just one example, but it happens far too frequently. The owner says that their dog will not hurt yours, just as he says that the dog just wants to play when he goes chasing sheep and other livestock.

The answer is a reliable recall and/or an instant drop on command – anywhere. It is often easier to get a dog to drop than to return. Bear in mind that once a dog sees something and decides to chase, he is focused on that thing, and that only. He probably does not even hear you shout, as his instinct to chase has taken over. An instant drop or recall can get you and your dog out of many a tricky situation. A dog who is lying down cannot fight another dog, chase a cat, bite a stranger or knock a child over. It is certainly the most important exercise you can teach your dog. Once taught, like most other exercises, it needs to be practised. Do not think that just because he did it last month, he will still do it tomorrow without a few reminders.

A properly socialised dog should not be aggressive towards strangers, children or other dogs. Adolescent dogs can become over-enthusiastic in their guarding, while the bitches may become rather nervous at this stage. In either case, enlist some help from friends. Having taught the dog to sit, now have your friend, armed with treats, come and knock on the door. Take the dog to the door, make him sit with the lead on, and ask your friend to offer the dog a treat. If your dog has been taught to shake hands, then have him do so with the visitor; dogs enjoy doing this, and it is much better than jumping up.

RECALL PROBLEMS

If your dog decides that it is great fun to run around in circles while you call him, it will certainly amuse passers-by, but not you! There are various things you can try. Whatever you do, do not shout or chase him, as this is just what he wants. Try calling him and walking or running away, tossing a ball or his favourite toy, or sitting down and ignoring him. Some people advocate crying, but we have never tried that and, whilst it might bring the dog to you, it might also attract some unwanted attention! When he does come, even if it takes half an hour, never grab him or scold him. You may feel like killing him but make a great fuss of him, praise him very well and give him a treat. Make him think it really was worthwhile coming to you.

BARKING IN CARS

A bad habit in dogs which is far too common is barking in cars. It is not only annoying, it is also dangerous. Some dogs bark while the car is moving – mostly Border Collies. They dash from side to side, looking at the traffic, and the fact that the driver manages to drive is a miracle. This habit should never have been allowed to develop, and, if it has, it must be stopped. You could try crating the dog; if he cannot see moving traffic, he may well be quiet. You might even throw a cover over the crate.

Some people have success with taking the dog out for short car rides on quiet roads. As soon as the dog barks at a vehicle, stop the car, grab the lead and rush the dog outside. Correct him verbally, grab him by the scruff and stare in his eyes while you tell him how bad he is. Do this every time he barks at a car until he gets the message. Once he lets a vehicle pass without barking at it, praise him well.

Dogs who bark while left in a parked car usually bark at passers-by or other dogs. Mary has a quick cure for this which you can try if you do not mind the local shoppers thinking you are crazy. She leaves the car with the dog in it, moves a short distance away and hides. Should the dog bark she rushes back, opens the door, grabs the dog and gives him a good ticking off. If she is further away and in a shop she still rushes out – the locals are used to it! This invariably works quite quickly. Our dogs do not bark at passers-by, but they do bark, and are encouraged to do so, if anyone stops and looks into the car or touches it.

CHEWING

We hear a lot about separation anxiety these days. Properly brought-up pups should have no problem being left alone for short periods, but teething can bring on this problem. The youngster's teeth may be worrying him, or he wants his owner, or he has nothing to do and he feels he just must chew something. Once again, a crate will be of help. If he is used to one, it should be no problem, and, if he is not, now is the time to get him used to one. Make sure he has something to chew that can stand chewing, such as a bone, a toy or a large, hard dog biscuit. Never go back to him when he is barking. Once he is quiet, go back and praise him, and maybe let him out for a game. Gradually leave him for longer and longer periods.

WHINING AND HOWLING

Some breeds are more prone to whining and howling than others. Most hounds howl at times, and, when they do, they simply do not hear you if you speak to or shout at them – they are in a world of their own. The only thing to do is to go up to the dog, grasp his muzzle and speak to him to get his attention. Tell him to be quiet, and then praise him when he obeys. Whining is an infuriating habit and should not be allowed to develop. It can be caused by frustration at being bored, and gun dogs have a tendency to whine. Not so long ago, most gun dogs would have been doing the job for which the breed was intended. Find him something else he can do. Stop him the same way as you would the howling, and do it the minute he starts, before it becomes a habit.

BEGGING

Some people complain that their dog begs at meal times. If you cannot teach your dog to lie down and behave, perhaps you should not have had a dog in the first place. Alternatively, shut him out of the room.

OVER-SEXED BEHAVIOUR

Some male dogs, especially the small ones, we find, become over-sexed on reaching maturity. They can be an embarrassing nuisance when they mount visitors' legs or, worse, grab hold of small children. If you do not intend using the dog at stud, then the simplest and best answer is to have him neutered. If you do not neuter him, then you must correct him very firmly immediately he shows signs of this behaviour.

NERVOUSNESS AND SHYNESS

Nervous dogs are a worry to themselves and to their owners, although there are some owners who enjoy having a nervous dog, because they invariably cling to their owners, which makes some owners feel good. It really depends how nervous the dog is. If he is genetically predisposed to nervousness (that is, his parents were nervous), then there is not a great deal which can or should be done. Most very nervous dogs have a pretty miserable life in today's noisy, crowded society. A dog who has had a bad fright can often, with time and care, be improved. It is a long and arduous task, worthwhile if the dog was originally of a good temperament. It is worth noting that most people who are bitten by dogs are bitten by nervous dogs.

Nervousness is often mixed with shyness. A shy dog, like a shy person, dislikes crowds, new environments, noise and strangers, until he gets used to them. The worst owner for the shy dog is the rowdy extrovert who crashes his way through life. The quiet, considerate owner can have an excellent relationship with a shy dog, by quietly encouraging him to accept what he considers to be scary situations.

PROFESSIONAL ADVICE

Problems in life are there to be overcome. We cannot always succeed, but in most cases it is well worth trying. The more you understand why your dog does certain things, the more you should be able to help him. If you find you are having little success, then it is best to seek professional advice.

Why is this little dog begging – is it for food or for a walk? You should know!
Photo: Sally Anne Thompson.

CHAPTER NINE

ASSISTANCE DOGS

The dog has probably served mankind for longer than any other animal, and it has certainly served him in more different ways. The number of tasks that dogs have been found capable of doing keeps increasing, until we sometimes wonder how many more uses for them are still to be found. Television has enabled many people to see guide dogs for the blind, hearing dogs for the deaf, dogs for the disabled, police dogs, sheep dogs and gun dogs carrying out their diverse tasks. While most viewers marvel at the abilities of these dogs, few have any idea how they are trained. In the belief that many readers will find this interesting as well as educational, we have been fortunate in obtaining contributions for Chapters Nine, Ten and Eleven from people who actually train dogs for these purposes.

GUIDE DOGS   By Neil Ewart

It may surprise many to learn that, unlike many other forms of dog training, the work of the guide dog is not based on any actual instinct. With other forms of dog training, much is based on the animal's innate need and desire to hunt. Thus, the stronger the hunting instinct, the better the dog.

There is no way that the guide dog can work out that his handler is visually impaired. To expect this is being totally unfair to the animal, and impedes the approach to his training and development. So what makes a good guide dog?

Friendly and easy-going, without too much initiative, the Labrador is ideally suited to its role as guide dog.

Photo courtesy: Guide Dogs for the Blind Association.

SUITABLE BREEDS

First, it is recognised that certain breeds have a higher success rate than others. Over the years, many breeds have actually qualified; however, while recognising this, it has been shown that the Labrador Retriever, Golden Retriever and the German Shepherd are generally the most successful.

Every dog that has ever lived will have his problems, although you may be forced to delve deep. The perfect dog – or human come to that – has never been born. So, when choosing any particular animal, you must balance any problem against his good qualities.

It is interesting that the Labrador is frequently crossed with the Golden Retriever in a bid to bring out desirable traits for guide dog work and to suppress those which are not desirable. The result is a medium-sized animal, consistently looking like a Labrador but with a slightly 'softer' temperament. Normally, they are very successful in the task for which they have been bred, but would not make good police or gun dogs due to their lack of any real drive.

The Labrador has a relatively short coat, which is easy to look after. It is of average size, which aids guiding, and, very importantly, it is socially very acceptable. Its temperament is generally very friendly and affable, without excessive initiative, which would be a problem. Remember that it is always necessary to be at least one step ahead of any dog. When you cannot see, this can sometimes prove difficult, so a dog that has a high level of drive and initiative can take advantage. Problems experienced with some of the breeds are over-excitability and greed! However, the Labrador's positive qualities far outweigh the difficulties.

The Golden Retriever has many of the advantages of the Labrador. In temperament, it can be a little more complex, with a sensitive nature which can be coupled with a stubborn streak. In this situation, it is vital that the handler can accurately identify when the dog is genuinely worried about a situation, as opposed to just digging his heels in!

The German Shepherd remains a favourite with many. Generally, its temperament is sound, and it does not seem to suffer as easily the stresses and strains of modern life. Perhaps this is because it is more of a 'thinking animal' than the gun dogs and often requires a greater rapport with its handler. Its long, striding gait can be a problem which can limit its suitability for visually impaired persons. However, the German Shepherd can be an easy dog to handle and look after.

TEMPERAMENT

Temperament is probably the most important trait in any potential guide dog. He has to be friendly and sound, as he will be meeting the public in busy urban areas every day of his life. Most dog handlers can

The Golden Retriever can be a little more complex, but with the right handler, a highly successful working relationship can be established.
Photo courtesy: Guide Dogs for the Blind Association.

anticipate events because they can see ahead. This is far more difficult if you have a problem with your sight, and it would be disastrous to have a guide dog with a questionable temperament.

Guide dog breeding programmes put temperament as their first priority. Studs and broods are all chosen from highly successful internal bloodlines. Of course, checks are made for possible hereditary problems, both physical and mental, and this will include both front and rear actions. Although these checks are very thorough, the very nature of breeding livestock tells us that problems will still appear. There is little doubt that the worst that could occur would be temperamentally unsound dogs being bred. This would include nervousness and any form of aggression.

Aggression, in any form, would be disastrous. There is no reason why a guide dog should not bark at the door, as long as his owner can make him desist on command. Members of the public, especially children, love to say hello to guide dogs, and breeding and training must produce dogs that do not object to this. There is a school of thought which says it could be a good thing for a guide dog to be capable of guarding his handler. However, it requires very little imagination to realise the potential dangers if this were the case. Therefore any dog which shows such traits will be withdrawn from training. No dog who does not make the grade is put down unless a vet diagnoses a very serious and incurable illness. Dogs that are insatiable hunters can be passed on to other organisations, such as the police, where the tendency, regarded as a fault for a guide dog, is a real asset.

CHARACTERISTICS

When breeding any dog, it is essential that the breeder sits down and works out what he, or she, is actually trying to produce. Is the dog for show, pet or working?. The latter, of course, includes guide dogs. So what characteristics are we trying to breed, if everything goes to plan?

The criteria are extensive, but below are a few examples of what is regarded as essential, and what may be merely desirable characteristics, in a guide dog. This will apply to the puppies produced and to their parents.

Essential: A sound temperament; physical soundness (hips, etc.); clear of any eye conditions, especially those known to be hereditary.

Desirable but not essential: Perfect dentition; perfect conformation and movement; a height to withers of 19ins – 23ins; general type for that particular breed.

Of no great importance: Coat colour and texture; eye colour; correct head and skull.

Anyone breeding for show winners, for example, will obviously add the last three points to their 'essential' list.

The German Shepherd Dog, the first breed to be used as a guide dog. The breed is still used, but is now in a minority.

Photo courtesy: Guide Dogs for the Blind Association.

In conclusion, a guide dog should fit the following description:
- Have a nice stable temperament with a happy, pleasing disposition.
- Should not be neurotic, shy or frightened.
- Reasonably energetic without being difficult to control.
- Not hyperactive, as this could cause problems to a handler who may be elderly or who may have additional health problems.
- Must not show any aggressive tendencies.
- Show low chasing instinct (one reason why collies are not too successful as guides).
- Able to concentrate for reasonably long periods.
- Not easily distracted, as this can break their concentration at a crucial moment.
- Willing to please and therefore enjoy his work.
- Confident with and tolerant of children.
- Confident with and tolerant of other animals.

- Responsive to the human voice.
- Not sound-shy and unlikely to go to pieces when, for example, a car backfires.
- Able to show 'reasonable' initiative without taking advantage.
- Not dominant or very self-interested.
- Able to change environment and/or handler without due stress.
- Within reasonable bounds of body sensitivity, therefore, not too tough or too soft.
- As free as possible from hereditary defects which could affect his work or well being.

This is achieved by:

Good breeding: Keeping very accurate records and only breeding from carefully selected stock. Breeding stock must not be bred from if it is proved that their offspring are not making the grade.

Good socialisation from birth to twelve months: Getting the puppy used to the sights and sounds of the big wide world as soon as possible.

Good training: Consistent and methodical handling, and ensuring that the dog definitely understands what is required and is praised effectively immediately he performs well; appropriate admonishment is given when he does not.

Good handling by the owner: Training the person and the dog together. Follow-up visits are made to the home every few months by qualified staff. This, hopefully, should prevent problems from building up and becoming irreversible.

It is worth reflecting that, as society changes its attitude to dogs and, perhaps, we all become a little more enlightened, all dog breeding should have soundness as an aim. There is no excuse for genetically temperamentally unsound dogs, be it for work or as pets. However, despite all the best efforts, breeding any living thing is partly a gamble as Mother Nature has a habit of playing unexpected tricks! This can catch out even the most conscientious and diligent breeder.

Few people realise that guide dogs do not have to be too intelligent. I do use this word with some hesitation, as the term 'intelligence' is easily misconstrued and means different things to different people. Possibly it is more accurate to say that a potential guide dog should not have too much initiative. You always have to be one step ahead of a dog, but some individual dogs demand that you need to be at least four!

The question that now arises is, if the training is not based on any instinct, then how does the guide dog learn?

The answer is surprisingly simple. The training is based on the dog's inherent desire to please the handler. A dog which is basically unresponsive to his trainer is normally not suitable. Therefore, by teaching the dog what is required, and consistently giving him the right incentives by accurate and effective use of praise and rebuke, the dog will happily do the job even though he does not actually understand why he is performing this way.

Incidentally, line up a qualified guide dog alongside any pet dog; try to spot the halo above either. It is very tempting to make the guide dog into something it is not and thereby expect too much from what is, after all, just an animal.

PUPPY WALKING

Firstly, guide dogs are bred for the desirable qualities. There are those who will argue that problem dogs (and humans) are so often the way they are because of their genes. Therefore, if you breed a problem it will always be there. The trait may be immediately evident, or it may be just under the surface.

When the puppy is about six weeks old, he needs to be socialised. This means being introduced to the world he is going to have to cope with throughout his life. This socialisation is vital for all dogs – guide dogs, police dogs, even pet dogs. It is very important to appreciate that good socialisation does not excuse bad breeding and is not a cure for a

Through the puppy-walking scheme, each guide dog puppy receives a comprehensive programme of socialisation in the first year of his life.
                    Photo courtesy: Guide Dogs for the Blind Association.

genetically unsound dog. However, a well-bred puppy that is properly socialised has every chance of being a pleasure to own.

During puppy walking, the young dog will be shown as many facets of life as possible. Once inoculated (the process starts at six weeks) the pup is put on a lead and taken out and about to meet people and to see unusual objects. Of course, the handler must be sensible and avoid situations where undue stress could be experienced. However, it also pays not to avoid letting the pup face up to 'life', and with a little

The guide dog must learn to negotiate obstacles allowing sufficient room for the handler.

Indicating at kerbs is an essential part of advanced training.

Photos: Alan Jones.

reassurance and confidence exhibited by the handler, most worries will be quickly dismissed.

TRAINING AND LEARNING

At about twelve months, the pup leaves his puppy walker for a specialist training centre, where he is introduced to more formal training. He continues to walk on the left-hand side of the handler and slightly ahead, as trained during the first twelve months. Tension on the lead should be moderate. The dog is introduced to the concept of walking in straight lines on pavements and only deviating to turn corners or to avoid obstacles. Over-handling at this stage can drive the more sensitive animal to favour the far left of the pavement, which means that moves over to the right become exaggerated and awkward.

He is also taught to indicate kerbs and steps by stopping and, usually, sitting. As his handler becomes confident and subsequently relaxed, he or she can actually 'feel' the upward movement of the dog's shoulders as he mounts the kerb.

It is extremely difficult to teach a dog that traffic is dangerous. Stray dogs that are seen dodging in and out of vehicles know that these hunks of metal can hurt. How do they know this? Almost certainly they have either been hit by a car or have had such a close shave that an association with discomfort has been established. Therefore reality has to be faced, and guide dogs should not be expected to make accurate judgements in particularly busy areas. The responsibility is on the handler to seek sighted help.

When the dog in training is confident with walking ahead, sticking to a reasonably straight line but weaving comfortably when appropriate, then the white harness is gradually introduced. It is really at this stage that the dog learns to accept the handler as an extension of himself. He judges distances between himself, the handler and obstacles on the right to allow enough room to pass without contact. Through a system of trial and error, habituation, and the formation of conditional reflexes, the dog learns to guide effectively.

Great patience is always required. Like all dog training, the handler must ensure that the dog actually understands commands before he can be corrected for any misdemeanour. Also, it is absolutely vital that the dog is praised effectively when he gets the task right. Since he wants to please, he must be given consistent and accurately timed incentives to work well. The dog's desire to please must not be diminished, as this remains the main incentive to work well. Throughout puppy walking and training the dog is not taught to retrieve, although a suitable toy may be used as play article. Retrieving skills are very important for, for example, a potential police dog. However, an obsessive retriever could actually be a liability when guiding a blind person, as they are likely to take off at the sight of children playing with a ball. Remember, life can be a lot easier when you have sight and can foresee problems ahead of you and take remedial action!

The dog must also be checked regularly by a vet. A dog that is unwell will not work as well as he should.

All guide dogs should enjoy a retirement. The average working life is about seven or eight years, so it is quite common for one to be retired at about 10 years and spend the rest of his days as a pet in the home of the person he guided for all that time.

HEARING DOGS   By Claire Guest

All owners are aware of the acuteness of their dog's hearing. Many report the pet dog who recognises his owner's footsteps or the sound of the car engine approaching.

Dogs do indeed have excellent hearing, better than any human's. Their range is greater, and they are able to detect sound at much higher frequencies than we can, hence the use of the special (silent to us) dog whistle. A dog's ability to discriminate between sounds is also excellent; a trained gun dog will pick out his owner's whistle from a number of similar-sounding whistles and return from a field away. Many dogs learn to distinguish the sound of their owner's car engine approaching the house from that of other approaching vehicles.

Hearing dogs are trained to become the ears of a deaf person, alerting them to a number of household sounds by touching them with a paw and then leading them, when asked, to the source. Hearing dogs are trained to respond to a variety of sounds including the alarm clock, doorbell/knock, telephone (deaf people use specially adapted telephones and minicoms), cooker timer and baby alarm. They can also be trained to fetch the deaf owner and to respond to the smoke alarm, firebell, or burglar alarm by alerting their owners with a paw and then dropping to the floor to indicate emergency.

TRAINING AND LEARNING

The training involves 'conditioning' the dog to a certain sound, and then training a number of responses in order to produce the finished result. It is an operant training programme – the correct behaviours are shaped, and a chaining of responses occurs so that the dog responds to the sound, fetches his owner and then leads him back to the correct sound source. The dog learns to respond to a number of sound stimuli and must discriminate between the sounds in order to make the correct

A hearing dog responds to sound and alerts his owner. He then leads his owner to the source of the sound.

Photo courtesy: Hearing Dogs for the Deaf.

response. For example, he must pick out the smoke alarm as a sound to which he must drop, but he must lead to a cooker timer. In addition to this, he must also discriminate between the owner's sounds and other sounds. For example, a dog who works in the office must discriminate between the recipient's phone and that of other work colleagues.

Training to sounds takes place at a specialist training centre, and takes four months after the young dog has completed his puppy socialising period. Dogs work to a maximum of 10 sounds. All dogs have an initial assessment to predict suitability, and then are placed with a volunteer socialiser where their progress is closely monitored. All dogs must have a temperament considered appropriate for an assistance dog, and must have trustworthy sociable natures.

It is understood that all breeds and types of dog with normal hearing have a comparable hearing range, and that therefore, from a purely auditory point of view, all dogs should work and train equally well. However, not all dogs make good hearing dogs. Most can be trained to perform the actual task of a hearing dog's work, that is, to touch and lead, but trainers of these dogs are aware that there is a clear difference between a dog that will touch and lead when awake and aroused, and a dog that will work well at other times.

QUALITIES

The qualities of a good hearing dog are not easy to define. Dogs that work well must bond closely to their deaf owner and they need a strong pack instinct. Independent dogs who do not bond well are rarely suitable. These dogs could be trained to work to command or cues when the handler is controlling the situation, but cannot be relied upon to work for a deaf owner consistently when the owner is unable to prompt the action in any way. Obviously, the deaf owner is unaware, for example, that the doorbell is ringing, and therefore could not command the dog to work.

There is often discussion as to whether the work of the hearing dog is a dominant role. It could be argued that the task is a dominant one because gaining the owner's attention by physical means, as many attention-seeking dogs do, with a paw, and then leading the owner who follows behind the dog, is dominant behaviour, and to some extent this may be the case. However, equally, the giving of the paw for a sound to elicit a reward could be considered to be juvenile behaviour, akin to the puppy-pawing that is used to request regurgitated food from adult dogs. One thing that is quite clear is that a hearing dog does not have to be a dominant dog, and that a submissive animal can be trained to perform the task efficiently. If the dog is assuming a dominant role for this task, this certainly does not lead to dominance-related problems.

This observation is supported by the findings of new research into canine pack hierarchy, which has indicated that an individual dog may assume the alpha role in one situation, but not necessarily in others. A naturally submissive dog can be trained to perform this task, and will take the initiative to work for the deaf recipient without any help or indication from the owner. Indeed, at times, as the deaf owner is unaware of sounds that may occur, they may unknowingly distract or ignore the dog. Training therefore teaches the dog to be confident and persistent about the response, and to reindicate a number of times if there is no reaction from the owner.

SUITABLE DOGS

One area about which very little is known is the reason why certain dogs appear to be more sound-aware or sound-sensitive than other dogs. Certainly, this is something noted from a behavioural point of view. When dogs are trained as hearing dogs, some animals appear to be more attuned to auditory stimuli, but it is unclear at present what might cause this difference. New research is showing that certain breeds have inherited hearing problems, but this cannot be the whole answer. Working-breed dogs may have strong working instincts that may detract the dog from hearing-dog work; for example, guarding breeds are rarely suitable, as they have a strong territorial instinct which makes them disinclined to leave the territory boundary, such as the front gate or door, which they must do to find the recipient and alert them to the sound. Terriers with strong hunting instincts may be distracted from their work by an animal in the garden, and hounds bred to hunt in packs follow ground scent and are rarely suitable.

A good hearing dog is generally a working crossbreed with no strong herding, guarding or hunting instinct which may cause distraction. An inquisitive, reasonably active dog is ideal. Many different breeds have been used as hearing dogs as they are not required to be any one particular size. It is possible to train a range of breeds not normally associated with assistance dog work. A number of toy breeds, including Chihuahuas and Papillons, have been successfully trained, and are very suited to more elderly recipients when exercise or space is limited.

All hearing dog training is based on positive association between sound and response. The hearing dog is not constantly alert or constantly working; for most of his time in the home, he may appear as an ordinary pet dog, lying in his bed or playing in the garden, but, when a household sound occurs, his behaviour will indicate his training. He will respond at any time of the day or night, as healthy dogs will, to the sound of the key in the door or the rattle of the lead.

It is a frequently asked question whether trained dogs out working learn to respond to other sounds in the home. The answer is that if they are rewarded for new responses, they will incorporate new sounds naturally. Some dogs tell their owners that the cat is mewing outside the back door, asking to come in; others, that the car alarm in the street is going. The hearing dog adapts, as all dogs do, to change in the environment, and will learn constantly.

Although rewards are used throughout the training procedure, trained dogs vary considerably with regard to how important the reward remains. Some always look forward to the food ration or special treat by the phone, others happily work for a cuddle and the natural rewards that emerge from hearing dog work: the person at the front door, the cake coming out of the oven that smells good. One aspect that is clear, however, is that dogs with different motivations can work equally well; the reason for working does not have to be the same in each dog to produce the finished result.

Hearing-dog training and the work of a hearing dog is unique, in that a trained dog will respond and work with no command, indication or direction from the handler. The hearing dog must have a real desire to respond as, once placed, the owner will be unaware of the sound stimulus. Training and selection ensure that the dogs are enthusiastic and happy workers. If they wait for a sound to occur it is with eager anticipation, whereas at other times, they live as normal members of the family pack.

BENEFITS

The benefits to deaf owners are immense. Many deaf people feel isolated from the hearing world and have difficulty relating to hearing people due to differences in language. Most born-deaf people use sign language, a complete language on its own, and may be unable to converse with hearing people who are unable to sign. The dog is able to communicate with them quickly, understanding their use of language and hand signals. This undoubtedly produces a strong bond between owner and dog, the deaf owner feeling that the dog understands them and that they are a partnership.

Owners who became deaf later in life and have to concentrate continuously in the company of other humans to lip read the conversation feel that their dog, who communicates non-verbally, is a kindred spirit. The placement of a hearing dog has been shown to reduce stress, and owners have reported feeling less depressed and anxious. The dog, with its pack instinct and strong bonding ability, gives a sense of well-being and companionship so often missed by deaf people in a hearing world. The hearing dog provides security, information, reassurance and comfort through both his specialised training and his natural instincts and behaviour. The first recipient to have a dog placed with her in Britain summed up this observation by saying of her hearing dog, Lady: "She has enriched my life beyond measure. She has dispelled my fears, brought me into contact with other people and her welcome seems to embrace the house itself; the silence and aloneness have gone."

DOGS FOR THE DISABLED   By Helen McCain

Dogs for the disabled are trained to perform tasks which disabled people find difficult or impossible to perform themselves, and, thereby enhance those people's levels of independence and mobility.

MAIN TASKS
Experience has shown that, whilst the range of disabilities is very wide, the number of tasks required for any one disabled person is likely to fall within the maximum of ten. The tasks most frequently demanded are:

- Retrieving accidentally dropped objects.
- Retrieving incoming mail and newspapers.
- Retrieving items delivered to the door.
- Retrieving specially adapted cordless telephones.
- Opening and closing doors.
- Turning lights on and off.
- Barking to raise an alarm.
- Acting as a steadier when rising from a chair or the floor.
- Providing momentum when walking for a disabled person with a balance problem, which requires the use of a harness and handle.

SUITABLE BREEDS
Whilst a large percentage of dogs for the disabled are Labradors,

A dog for the disabled is trained to carry out a multitude of domestic tasks, and can also act as a steadier when the owner rises from a chair.

Photo courtesy: Dogs for the Disabled.

Golden Retrievers or Labrador/Golden Retriever crosses, many other breeds have also proved successful, both pedigree and crossed, including Collie/Spaniel and Collie/Golden Retriever crosses, German Shepherds, Standard Poodles, a Portuguese Water Dog and a Finnish Lapphund.

Whilst taking into consideration the amount of care a particular breed needs from its owner, how publicly acceptable the dog is and the likely length of the breed's working life, the breed's general levels of willingness, responsiveness, adaptability, concentration, suspicion, self-interest and so on also have to be considered. These characteristics all play a part in how a dog reacts in different situations, whether influenced by instinct or by an external factor, such as humans.

SUPPLY

Most of the puppies trained as dogs for the disabled are bred specifically for the work. However, dogs from other dog organisations are occasionally suitable; the dog may have been withdrawn from training for a reason specific to that work. In particular, dogs who proved unsuitable as guide dogs for the blind have been successfully trained as dogs for the disabled, as there is a similarity in the selection. Both types of work require breeds which are adaptable, very willing, able to concentrate and so on – such as Labradors and Golden Retrievers.

Occasionally, careful selection has provided some suitable working stock from other sources, such as rescue centres, pet homes and breeders. However, experience has shown that a puppy-walking scheme is the most successful means of providing a source of suitable stock, and, ultimately, enabling an organisation to breed for the behaviour and temperament required in a dog for the disabled.

PUPPY WALKING

The puppies are looked after by puppy walkers from approximately six weeks of age until they are twelve or fourteen months old, depending on the individual puppy's level of maturity. The puppy walkers are responsible for providing the puppy with invaluable socialisation within as many different environments and situations as is practically possible.

Whilst not actually training the puppy, the walker will encourage all instinctive behaviour that could be shaped by an experienced instructor at a later date to achieve a particular task, such as fetching and retrieving a toy or playing tug of war with an old towel or toy. The walker encourages the puppy's confidence to explore in unusual environments, cupboards, undergrowth and so on.

ASSESSMENT

Whether a dog has been puppy-walked, or come from an outside source, they are all assessed for thirty days when they arrive for training.

This can be the most important stage of a dog's training because it allows the handler to observe the dog's own natural behaviour, without it having been influenced by training or by an established relationship with his trainer.

During the course of the assessment the dog will be introduced to many different environments, both rural and urban, such as the countryside, parks, water, railway stations, towns and schools.

Noting a dog's reactions in these different locations and their response to simple tasks, such as basic obedience, will allow the trainer to form an educated evaluation of a dog's suitability for particular tasks.

REWARD TRAINING

To ensure that the high standard of work achieved during training is maintained once the dog is with his new owner, the most effective training has proven to be positive, reward-based training.

High willingness in the dog develops into a desire to please his handler and receive praise, either verbal or a random tidbit reward. Few owners are able to praise or admonish their dogs physically due to the limitations of their conditions, so voice control is essential.

During the early stages of training, food rewards are used to enhance verbal praise, and then this is made more random as the training progresses. To ensure a successful change of handler from the dog's trainer to the new owner, food rewards are reintroduced initially, to help to clarify the dog's understanding of his new owner's control. They are eventually reduced until they are given randomly, as the relationship between the dog and his new owner develops.

TASK TRAINING

The many different tasks that dogs for the disabled perform are all based around natural, instinctive behaviour common to all dogs, shown to a greater or lesser degree in different breeds and individuals. To develop a dog's desire to respond, play situations are created to test his reaction and likely suitability for training in the different areas.

RETRIEVING

Play retrieving with toys of various materials develops the dog's confidence to pick up more unusual items. A play item made out of cloth and placed in a box will encourage a dog to fetch clothes out of a washing machine. Dumbbells made of materials such as wood, plastic, rubber and metal develop the dog's confidence with different textures.

Once the dog has picked up a toy, he is encouraged to follow the trainer around with the toy still in his mouth before it is taken off him, which tests his ability to carry items such as milk crates, and his likely response to the "hold" command, once introduced.

Following this play situation, the dog's trainer is then in a good position to be prepared for the likely response to the formalisation of the exercise. This involves having the dog in a controlled position on a lead and collar. The trainer offers the dog a dumbbell, and the command "hold" is introduced when the article is held cleanly at the front of the dog's mouth and positioned behind the canines. Any mouthing or movement of the article in the dog's mouth is discouraged by a short, sharp, verbal admonishment and a display of visual dissatisfaction, if appropriate.

Once a satisfactory hold response is achieved the exercise can be moved on through the different stages, including "fetch", "come", "thank you", reinforced by verbal praise or a food reward.

TUG OF WAR

Playing 'tug of war' games and allowing the dog to win, if appropriate, develops the initial understanding of the word "pull" and develops his confidence under such situations rather than the killing instinct, seen when the dog shakes his head.

As the dog's confidence and understanding increase, the trainer starts to make the situation more realistic by encouraging the dog to pull on a door or cupboard drawer handle. The dog continues to get the satisfaction of winning the game when he receives praise from his handler on opening the door.

Once the response is established, the dog's handler could be positioned at one end of the room and, on the command "pull the door", the dog will independently go and open the door, using an appropriate attachment fitted to the handle.

TARGETING

Many pet dogs will use their paws to pat an owner for attention or to create a positive response from someone, such as offering to shake hands. You can also see dogs using their paws to get toys out of difficult places, like under a cupboard, or to hold the dinner bowl still while licking it clean. All of these responses are common, and can be used to teach a dog such tasks as switching lights on and off or pressing a button to call a lift. Developing a dog's need to have a role by teaching him to "give a paw" when meeting members of the public can be adapted to "give a paw to the light" or "give a paw to the lift". The words, *give*, *paw*, *lift* and *light* are recognised as words of command.

Utilising the dog's desire to please and to create a role for himself within his pack will help to maintain a satisfactory standard of work in these areas, despite the fact that the dog is often working independently, with limited support from his handler – for example, having to locate a phone left in a room in another part of the house.

STABILITY

During the initial assessment, some dogs are occasionally found to be unsuitable for the different needs of the task work. However, stability work still satisfies the dog's need for a role, and, following a physical assessment for health and fitness, the dog can be trained to provide stability and an appropriate level of forward tension, which assists in maintaining an individual's walking position and momentum.

The dog's natural ability to care for another pack member enables this assistance to be successful, while retaining the handler's position of pack leader by controlling the dog through obedience and directional commands.

SUMMARY

The provision of dogs for the disabled is a recent development, but many new types of assistance have already been successfully used. Experimentation and experience can only lead to more areas of work and assistance in this vast field.

CHAPTER TEN

WORKING DOGS

The dog is not 'almost human' – thank goodness! He can carry out many tasks of which man is quite incapable; even in this age of technology, we do not always understand how he does it. It is important to remember, however, that no dog is capable of carrying out any of these tasks without the help of a human leader. It must be a partnership between man and dog – master and servant, who usually become very good friends.

HERDING DOGS   By John Holmes

The first use to which man put the dog was to help him to hunt and to catch his food. Dogs are still used for hunting, but, in most parts of the world very little of the quarry they catch is used for food. If it were not for the sheepdog, the production of wool and mutton in Europe and in the wide open spaces of the New World countries would be an uneconomical proposition. If it had not been for the wolf's instinct to hunt, we would have no sheepdogs as we know them today.

It may surprise some readers to learn that there are hundreds of dogs working on farms who have never had any real training. They gather flocks and move them from one place to another, and, if a sheep breaks

The working sheepdog follows his instinct while remaining under the control of his handler.

Photo: Keith Allison.

away, they quickly turn it back into the flock. If they get it wrong they are cursed or have a stick thrown at them, but they are never shown how to get it right. Dogs, like their owners, are better educated today than in days gone by, but there are still many dogs on farms who could be described as entirely self-taught. Furthermore, they do not learn by watching another dog, as some people would have us believe. They simply follow an instinct derived from the wolf's hunting instinct and diverted, very slightly, by man's careful, selective breeding over hundreds of years. It is important to remember that, while intelligence plays a big part in *how* a dog works, it plays no part at all in *why* a dog works. The dog does not say to itself "This pack leader of mine can't run nearly as fast as I can, so I will please him a lot if I gather these sheep and bring them to him." A well-bred young dog who has never seen a sheep may be taken into a field where there are sheep and let off the lead. Without any command or encouragement from the owner, the dog is likely to take off and run around the sheep, especially if they run away. It does not always happen like that, but in many cases it does.

On the other hand, a pup will sometimes follow a shepherd on his

A strong-eyed dog should be able to work any type of stock.

Photo: Keith Allison.

daily rounds and show no interest at all in the sheep, even when another dog is working. Then, one day, quite suddenly and for no apparent reason, the young dog takes off and runs around the sheep.

He will probably gather the sheep into a bunch and run around and around rather than bringing them to the handler, but this is the beginning, the foundation of all sheepdog training. Until and unless a dog does this, there are few sheepdog trainers who will bother to teach him anything else.

It should be noted that we have in mind the Border Collie, only one of the many breeds of sheepdog. It is, in fact, the newest breed of sheepdog, and the name was unknown until the 1920s. The breed originated in the Border Counties of Scotland and England, and the dogs were originally known as 'creepers' or 'strong-eyed' dogs. It is this strong eye that distinguishes the breed from other sheepdogs. Of course, the breed did not suddenly arise from nowhere. It is really a strain, originally evolved from the various Collie types, which have been herding sheep since prehistoric times. When it was realised that, in sheepdog trials, 'strong-eyed' dogs were invariably more successful than 'loose-eyed' ones, breeders, not surprisingly, bred for this trait.

They also wanted dogs that were very keen to work – in other words, possessing a very strong herding instinct. By careful selective breeding, and not a little inbreeding, a new breed has been produced which has what can only be described as an over-developed, abnormal herding instinct. That breed has become known as the Border Collie, and is now a recognised breed by the Kennel Clubs, with classes at dog shows.

In the *Book of the Dog*, published in 1948, James A. Reid, the first Secretary of the International Sheepdog Society (ISDS), wrote: "here we are concerned only with the working Collie long known simply as 'the Collie' or as the 'Scottish Collie' and nowadays popularly, but erroneously, as the 'Border Collie'."

Sheepdog trials started in 1873, and in 1906 the ISDS started a stud book for working Sheepdogs. It is interesting that, since then, quite a number of Bearded Collies have been registered, some having been successful in trials. These are strong-eyed dogs, and they work in exactly the same way as the more usual 'Border Collie' type.

The only other breed that works in this way is the Australian Kelpie. This is the only breed we know of which competes successfully against the Border Collie in Sheepdog trials. It originated from working Collies taken from Scotland by settlers to Australia. One of the first of these was an in-whelp bitch called Kelpie (Gaelic for water sprite), a phenomenal worker, who became the foundation of the breed. This means that the Border Collie and the Kelpie share a common ancestry. Strangely enough, so do the Rough and Smooth Collies seen in the show ring.

The superiority of the Border Collie for most types of work with sheep is proven by the fact that it can be found in every country in the world where sheep are grazed. However, it is not universally popular with farmers and shepherds. They keep them because of the difficulty of finding good old-fashioned working Collies, and because if they keep a bitch, the pedigree puppies are worth much more. On hills where gorse and bracken are prevalent, a strong-eyed dog can creep around without the sheep even noticing him. If such a dog suddenly comes across an old ewe, she may just stand and stare at him. Some of today's dogs have so much 'eye' that they simply stand and stare back! This does not endear the dog to a farmer or shepherd with a lot of work to do and limited patience.

On the bracken-infested areas of the West Highlands of Scotland, 'Hunters' have always been used for 'gathering'. These are noisy dogs, often old-fashioned Beardies, who drive the sheep out of their hiding places. In recent years, quite a number of New Zealand Huntaways have been imported into the UK. These are much bigger than Border Collies, very noisy, and they keep barking while they are running. They are not for the connoisseur sheepdog enthusiast, but they do get on and do the job, and are popular with those who own them.

OTHER BREEDS

There are other breeds of sheepdog in various parts of the world. Some, like the German Shepherd, are better known as police dogs, but they do work sheep in Germany and have their own trials. Other sheepdogs do not herd at all but have been bred for centuries to guard flocks in Europe. These include the Komondor and Pyrenean, which are proving very successful in America as a deterrent to attacks by coyotes. The pups are reared with the sheep and stay with the flock on their own, night and day.

There are enough breeds and types of dogs working sheep and cattle in all parts of the work to fill a book. The common mistake is to believe that the Border Collie is the only one.

SEARCH AND RESCUE DOGS   By Neville Sharpe

The natural instincts of a dog are motivated by two basic requirements – food, to ensure that he has adequate food and can survive; and reproduction, to regenerate the species by breeding. It is a general assumption, proven by fact, that wild animals work best when they are hungry and thus start to hunt for food. There is no doubt that when an animal is hungry, the olfactory glands in the nose are increased in sensitivity, giving the best possible working conditions. This may be adopted in the case of a search dog who is taught to work on smell, and, for this reason, it is not wise to work a dog with a full stomach who may produce a reduced scent efficiency factor.

SCENT

Scent is a sense in animals that we have very little chance of surpassing. The ability of an animal to smell, detect and identify air smells is quite incredible – wild animals can detect danger over a distance of miles on the African plains. Domesticated animals can identify friend or foe, or whether the food offered is acceptable or distasteful.

The theory of scent is wide and complex, but, for practical purposes, scent may be divided into broad categories of wind or airborne scent and ground scent.

Wind scent is the name given to the scent which attracts the dog in searching. It is airborne scent from an individual or object, and may, in the former case, be described as the personal odour from the body of the person concerned. The amount of personal odour varies according to that person's constitution, health, clothing, nourishment, activity, mental condition and state of cleanliness. It is greatly intensified when there is physical exertion. In the case of objects, the scent may be a characteristic of the object, or it may be the result of some human contact. The scent of the article itself may be alien to the particular ground on which it lies, such as a piece of sawn or broken wood lying on grassland.

The dog using its acute sense of smell becomes alert to the odours detected through his nose onto his olfactory glands. The degree of discernment varies with the rate of evaporation, air movement and the type of country over which the scent is set up. Quite obviously, the most important feature affecting scent from an operational point of view is time. The more quickly a dog can be brought to follow a scent, the more successful the result is likely to be.

Scent is subject to evaporation and is therefore greatly affected by climatic conditions. Generally speaking, the most favourable conditions are either mild, dull weather, or when the temperature of the ground is higher than that in the air (normally at night), or in areas where the ground is sheltered.

Factors which adversely affect scent are hot sunshine, strong winds and heavy rainfall after the scent has been set up.

Frost and snow may have either the effect of preserving or destroying a scent, depending on whether this occurs before or after the scent has been occasioned.

As I have already said, scent is a wide and complex subject. There will be innumerable occasions when the accepted theories are contradicted by the dog's ability and willingness to follow a scent which, under the conditions, should be non-existent. The only true test is for the dog to be given the opportunity to establish whether or not working conditions prevail.

MOUNTAIN RESCUE SEARCH DOGS

Mountain rescue search dogs carry out a very important function within rescue work. They are highly trained to quarter and search extensive areas on the mountains. They are taught to search for and locate human scent. Scent discrimination technique is not used, however; they are trained to locate any human scent. It is generally

The mountain rescue search dog must quarter and search extensive areas of mountainside, and locate human scent.

found in operational circumstances that, invariably, by the time someone is reported missing in the mountains, most other walkers and hikers have in fact returned, leaving only the reported missing casualties on the mountains.

Over the years, many different breeds of dogs have been used. German Shepherds, Labradors, Spaniels, Retrievers, Pointers and, of course, the traditional Border Collie farm dog. In more recent times, there has been a distinct move towards the Border Collie, and it goes without saying that these dogs are bred specifically by farmers for herding and gathering sheep.

TRAINING

How are these dogs prevented from gathering sheep, when they have been bred over many years to do so? There is no doubt that inbreeding produces very good prodigies, and the natural instinct is to gather and herd. Can that instinct ever be controlled or overruled? The answer is that it can – up to a point.

In the early stages of training, it is essential that the dog is provided with another direction in his life – not only in his family bond, but also in his training. This must be directed towards the social and working atmosphere of people, and the dog should learn to derive an enormous amount of pleasure from sharing his life with humans. There is no doubt that, to change the lifestyle of any dog, many aspects of his upbringing need to be thought out very carefully. In the case of a search dog, it would be futile to allow him to come into contact with livestock in the first few months of his life. It is, however, important to allow the dog to identify with stock, and to be put through a negative training programme in later months, as the dog matures.

We must remember that, during the lifetime of a dog, we cannot promise him anything. An animal lives for that moment in time. Only by routine can we train the animal to understand a pattern of life – exercise, playing, rewarding and feeding at regular intervals. It is generally accepted that the most impressionable age for learning is between three and nine months.

There is much to be gained from acquiring a puppy and training it to your way of life and to become accustomed to your environment. The dog should be able to maintain his natural ability to work, whilst being influenced by his handler's training to respond to his commands. This should not lead to compulsive training, but should be a game of pleasure, and there should not be a tremendous distinction between the two. During this period of life, any bad habits which are allowed to develop will generally remain with that dog for the rest of his life. This can be quite a worrying prospect to many, and, all too often, owners fail to take advice before the habit is well-established in the dog's mind. It goes without saying that the acquisition of an older dog may result in inheriting the problems already planted in the dog's mind.

It is important in dog training to remember that the handler must always remain the pack leader, both in the domestic and in the training environment. All dogs will follow the pecking order, and rising up the hierarchy will always be on the dog's mind.

In the early stages of training a search dog, we have to establish some basic ground rules. The pack leader must always be the handler. There must be a set programme of events, preferably taking place at the same location each day, based purely on the fact that training is simply repetitive practise carried out in such a manner that the dog eventually learns the exercise, willingly carries out that exercise, and improves with time.

The training programme will follow a pattern. This is achieved by replacing the natural instinct of gathering with a programme of training which is more appealing to the dog – a game involving close contact with people, involving chasing, searching and locating. Only by many hours of training can we establish some other basic ground rules in the dog's mind. The motivating factors must be the will and love of the dog to work for his master, and his desire to enjoy and gain pleasure from the rewards offered by the handler when he is successful.

It is important in any training that there is a distinct incentive for the dog to work. This can be a reward of food, play or just affection. All dogs are different; it would be wrong to say what is correct or even acceptable to your own dog. One thing I can say is that, without some positive sharing between handler and dog, progress becomes difficult, at times impossible, and motivation is extremely hard.

Generally speaking, we have to encourage dogs to play, chase and retrieve. Not all dogs have a natural ability, and some find it quite hard to follow. It is desirable that the dog is encouraged as a puppy to play with and enjoy a 'play toy' of whatever variety you may wish. It is acceptable to use anything so long as it provides motivation and a sense of enjoyment for the dog.

In the early stages of training a working dog, the exercise is based on the retrieve. Once a dog becomes possessive with its 'play toy', we begin to play 'cat and mouse' with it – we steal it and run away and hide with it, and this instinctively encourages the dog to chase, seek and find. This is the very basic lesson in teaching a dog to search. The exercise is advanced in such a manner that, eventually, the dog no longer sees the 'thief' disappear with his property, but has to start and hunt for it himself. Progress is fast, and the dog is always rewarded with episodes of playing with his handler and, of course, the 'play toy'.

Teaching the dog commands, accompanied by words of encouragement, is most important from the start. This exercise is generally carried out working into the wind, and very quickly the dog starts to use its nose and detection becomes easy. Progress is made by moving the dog solely on to a human target, and using the play toy or food as a reward to imprint the exercise in the dog's mind.

INDICATING

Eventually the dog will indicate human scent, working on the wind and, as the exercise advances, in different areas, moving on to more difficult ground and obstacles. The time factor is also extended, slowly introducing an extension of time between the start of the search and the 'find'. It is often at this point that we start to appreciate the natural out-run ability of the Border Collie – a dog bred to work in the hills, possessing endless amounts of energy and a tremendous passion to work. All these attributes now give us the ability to master a dog initially bred to gather sheep and to fine-tune him to carry out another type of duty.

The most essential part of the training is teaching the dog how to indicate the fact that he has located a scent source (the casualty). Some of the major difficulties handlers experience in the mountains whilst engaged on operational duties are remoteness, the darkness of night searches and, of course, adverse weather conditions. These factors have, over many years of learning, taught us that we must teach the dog to return to the handler once he has located the missing casualty, and then indicate by barking the fact that he has located the scent source.

Many weeks are spent ensuring that this find sequence is practised to perfection. The major move forward onto quartering and searching does not allow time for returning to basics. Although in any training it may be that a simpler exercise may be introduced because of some failure, it is most important that all search dogs have a very strong and positive indication.

As time moves on – and the above training may well take some six months – we would expect the dog to advance into searching technique, to enable him to quarter and search and to be capable of being directed by the handler to any location. This will eventually be many hundreds of yards away.

As the indication becomes strong, it is not uncommon for the dog to return to the casualty before the handler arrives. A pattern may develop whereby the dog will go back and forth between casualty and handler until the handler arrives at the casualty's position. It goes without saying that a trained dog can cover the ground incredibly quickly, at times making the handler look comparatively slow. However, as a team, they are exceptionally proficient, and records show that, through their speed and tenacity, they have saved many lives.

Throughout this demanding programme, reward and praise will dominate the exercises. Encouragement and support from the handler will drive the dog on. At times, they will be separated in their work by the nature of the hills, gullies, crags and ravines. Support to the dog by verbal command and praise is important. This may also be supplemented by a whistle or hand-signals when working at distances, to help guide the dog through the areas being searched.

The combination of a good dog and handler is a pleasure to see. The successful completion of two years' hard work is for assessment to result in the dog being placed on the search and rescue dog call-out list.

PRAISE

Animals enjoy praise, just as humans do. This is the one available and practical incentive we can offer when training a dog. But what is praise? It involves placing a value on your dog in a very practical sense. It comes from body language, eye contact, the physical stroking and fussing, playing with the dog on his 'level', food, and finally, the sheer love and devotion which must be displayed to him in a manner in which he understands. He does not understand language, but thrives on routine; and remember, an obedient dog is a healthy dog. He lives for this moment in time – not later, but now. That is why routine helps him to put things into perspective on a daily basis – he identifies and associates those occasions when he is going to work or is simply out for a walk.

Praise must always be administered at the right time, so that the dog can learn to understand the association between the exercise and the praise. The praise should come freely and enthusiastically, and with a degree of understanding between dog and man. The dog must see that it provides a lasting, learning and praising conclusion to the exercise. This all requires concentration on the part of the handler, and allows little time for 'sightseeing' whilst training. Giving praise is an art in itself, and not all handlers are gifted with the natural talent. However, careful understanding and practice will enable the handler to improve these skills and ensure that the dog is not confused, but instead feels supported when asked to complete an exercise.

There are many different opinions on how to praise a dog, with many people quite naturally regarding their own successful method to be the best. However, this tendency should be avoided and you should remain open to all possibilities. Remember that a dog does not care about our opinion; he simply reacts to a situation in his own individual manner. We should always be open to any method which may produce the right results

PLAY AND FOOD

As dog owners, we should always be aware that many of our actions are rewarding to our dogs without us even being aware of it. As a result of these actions, you may find that you are inadvertently training your dog to do the wrong thing. This can also happen if the dog is incorrectly punished for his behaviour at the wrong time. There is no doubt that to reward a dog in play or by giving food is a very happy occasion for an animal. This action is always very easy, but we should remember that, in progressive training, the dog's overall impulse to please should, in fact, come from the exercise itself and not always for the reward at the completion of the exercise.

Moreover, it is very habit-forming to reward a young dog with food on a regular basis, as this takes his mind off what is actually being taught. Some dogs, of course, do not always want to play at the end of an exercise. In most cases, words of praise should be sufficient. The rule to be applied is that, providing you achieve results and the dog understands what is being taught, a balance of different types of praise must be applied.

PERFORMANCE VALUE

This term generally implies that the dog experiences so much pleasure and enjoyment from the exercise itself that he will perform it willingly, quickly and certainly for his own pleasure. The dog's response to the "Find" is often excitement, and clearly, this is an ideal end-result, bringing together the completion of the trained exercise and the ultimate reward for the dog – finding the missing person.

INSTINCT

Finally, a reminder of the importance of instinct. Instinct is a very strong factor in all animals. It cannot be removed, it will always remain foremost in a dog's character and make-up. However, with gentle persuasion and the correct training, a dog can be taught many things, and, without instinct, this would not be possible.

POLICE DOGS   By Dr Peter Storey

Today, there are some highly trained police dogs from a host of breeds, including mongrels, who are assisting the police in their very difficult primary functions of preventing, detecting and fighting both crime and terrorism, and, of course, assisting in the more passive roles of searching for lost persons, and, indeed, providing good public relations for the police at schools and other public organisations.

It can be seen that, in order to fulfil such requirements, it takes a very special type of dog, whether it be a German Shepherd, normally used for general-purpose patrol work, or, indeed, a smaller breed of dog used in specialist searching for explosives and drugs.

THE PERFECT POLICE DOG

The perfect working police dog is very difficult to find, and more and more police Forces are being forced, at great expense, to commence their own breeding programmes to satisfy their needs for suitable dogs.

The ideal dog has a sound temperament, neither nervous nor aggressive, but courageous, a dog who approaches the unknown with gentle curiosity, or sometimes mischievousness, a dog who is sound both physically and mentally; but, above all, a dog who can utilise his superior senses of scent and hearing to enhance his above-average instincts of retrieving, hunting, play and protection, to assist his trainers in teaching him to track, search and bite in a controlled manner.

The dog is somewhat of a mystery, in that it is the only animal in the world with an instinctive desire to co-operate with man. No other animal has established such a mental understanding with man. If we can understand to some degree this desire, and understand their willingness to please us, we can harness their superior senses and instincts to assist us in our primary functions in a way that no electric gadget can.

So how are the instincts of our canine friends utilised to assist in this difficult task?

TRACKING

As any police officer, or, indeed, civilian handler will tell you, to handle a good tracking dog is 'heaven' – the culmination of many months or years of persuasive training.

A tracking dog must use his sense of smell to locate hidden persons or property. An above-average retrieve instinct is considered an asset.

Photo courtesy: The Metropolitan Police.

Tracking is the ability of a dog to track down hidden persons or property using his sense of smell. All good tracking dogs have one thing in common – an above-average retrieve instinct. This is not to say that a dog without above-average retrieving instinct cannot be trained to track; indeed, that is not true. There are varying methods of teaching a dog to track, but the natural way is to use the retrieve instinct to train the dog to track as a play exercise. This way, the dog enjoys his work and tends not to tire so easily.

How do we know whether a dog has above-average retrieve instinct? The system that I have used over the last 20 years is tried and tested. First of all, the dog is taken to a wood or copse away from its home environment. The reason I do this is to test the dog's boldness at the same time as the retrieve instinct. It sometimes helps if the dog's former owner or handler is present to throw the dog's favourite toy into deep vegetation. The dog is allowed to see the toy being thrown, held for a minute and then released. I would expect the successful candidate to plough boldly into the vegetation and search for its toy, not giving up until it is found. The exercise may take 10 or 15 minutes, but the enthusiasm to search must remain and the animal should not tire if it is fit.

There is an exception to this rule, in that a dog may possess the qualities that we are looking for but may not have been socialised correctly as a puppy. Maybe he has never been taught to play, and the instinct has not surfaced yet. In this case, a good instructor will recognise the problem and allow the animal more time to show its full potential.

However, experience has shown that dogs who have been socialised correctly, and played with from an early age, make the best tracking and searching dogs. It comes as second nature to them to search diligently and enthusiastically for long periods, whilst thoroughly enjoying the exercise.

The tracking exercise is merely an extension of the dog's hunting and retrieving instincts to look for and find a play article. In the initial stages, the dog is introduced to a pasture or playing field with reasonably short grass which has not been trodden on or mown recently. This is to make sure that the only scent produced by crushing the vegetation is made by the track layer, and so there is no confusion for the dog. The handler holds the dog whilst the trainer walks away with the animal's toy. The dog is allowed to see the plaything secreted in the grass some yards away, and then allowed to run forward on the lead, with the handler in fast pursuit behind it. When the dog finds the toy, the lead comes off and play commences with as much enthusiasm as possible. This is a play exercise and should always remain that way. The training exercise is repeated several times, the distance between the dog and the toy increasing gently. At this stage, the dog is using his hunting instinct to find his toy. His head is in the air and he is looking for the toy. What we must now do is train the dog to put his nose down and track for the play article. This is achieved by making the track both longer and older so that the scent coming off the grass is less volatile. The dog soon learns that, to achieve his objective, he must resort to using all of his senses over varying terrain.

Very gentle progress is made over a period of weeks, the track becoming more and more difficult to follow, but the main ingredient should always remain fun! Every exercise must be successful, which it should be, if the dog's instinct was assessed correctly in the initial stages.

SEARCHING

This is the training of the dog to find hidden property, persons, explosives and drugs.

Assessment of a potential search dog is similar to that of a tracking dog, and he should display the same qualities, and, in particular, an above-average retrieve instinct.

If a dog possesses such qualities, it is an easy task to train him to search for and find hidden property upon which human scent has been placed. The exercise is self-explanatory, and the only thing we must teach is 'retrieve to hand' or to indicate by barking if the article is too big to retrieve.

Strangely enough, a similar method can be used to teach a dog to search buildings and open countryside for hidden persons, whether those persons are lost or hiding. This method has been used to great effect in training a dog to confidently search in a non-aggressive manner.

Again, the handler holds the dog on a lead, and the trainer holds the dog's toy in front of them. The dog is encouraged to bark for the toy and is immediately given it as a reward. The dog is then allowed to see the trainer run into a building holding the toy, and dog and handler follow almost immediately. When the dog (who is still on the lead) finds the trainer, he is encouraged to bark for his toy and, of course, is given it with great praise.

It really is then a question of making the exercise more and more

A sniffer dog in training. A play article, containing the substance to be found, is used in a variety of search and retrieve situations.

Photo: The Rugby Advertiser.

The dog must work under the control of the handler, but the handler must have total confidence in the dog's ability.

Photos courtesy: The Metropolitan Police.

difficult over a period of weeks, eventually hiding the trainer away from sight completely to encourage the dog to use his nose as opposed to using his eyes only.

The training of specialist dogs to seek out explosives and drugs is very complex, and cannot be explained in a short paragraph. However, the principle of using the retrieve instinct remains constant. A perforated plastic pipe containing the substance to be found becomes the dog's play article, which is hidden away in the presence of the dog. The dog is released and, upon finding the article, is played with and praised. At no time does the dog come into direct contact with any substance found, and is certainly never allowed to become reliant to any degree on it.

We still do not understand just how a dog's olfactory system works. The average German Shepherd has about 220 million olfactory sensory cells, compared with a human's five million, and one might jump to the conclusion therefore that a dog's sense of smell is forty-four times better than man's. However, this is not the case, as I am reliably informed that the results from an olfactometer suggest that the dog's sense of smell is one million times better, but, above all, they have the ability to discriminate between the ingredients of a scent.

This makes the training for explosives and drugs difficult in the early stages because, as far as we know, the dog could be searching for the plastic pipe ingredient of our play article, and not the substance itself. In an experiment, the four ingredients of an explosive were secreted in separate, sterile rooms, and four fully-trained explosives-search dogs were sent to each room to search. Three out of four dogs indicated a different ingredient and ignored the rest, but, when all ingredients were placed together and secreted, all four dogs found the substance. Interesting.

As a result, it is important for the play article containing the substance to be removed as early as possible and replaced by the new explosive (not inert) or drug. When the dog finds the hiding spot, a play article is 'palmed' into the hide by the handler, and the dog is then played with and praised.

Teaching a dog to bite is an extension of the play instinct. As the dog becomes more confident, an element of discipline is introduced.

Photo: The Rugby Advertiser.

THE HANDLER

To train a dog to find any substance is easy; it takes minutes with the correctly-assessed dog – but training the handler to 'read' the dog is another matter. All dogs have different temperaments and characters, and, of course, they both search and indicate in different ways. The handler must learn to stand back during search exercises and allow the dog to work independently. Having said that, he must always have his dog in view, and learn to recognise any change in the dog's behaviour. Should the dog show more interest in a certain area, he must have the presence of mind to remain standing back, and allow the dog to sort out the problem himself. Too many inexperienced handlers jump in too soon to assist their charge and, as a result, prompt a false indication from the dog, who, of course, rushes to please him! One of the biggest tasks the instructor has is to teach the handler to have confidence in his dog's ability; after all, the dog is the one with the superior senses, and that is why he is employed to assist the police.

Training is full of pitfalls, and it is important that a fully-qualified instructor is always present to nip any problems in the bud before they become irreversible. The handler must learn to read his dog when he is obviously giving positive indication. Is it convection of air, wind direction, draughts or other turbulence causing the indication? It has been known for a dog to indicate a substance on the opposite side of the room due to air convection! All of these phenomena must be taken into account when attempting to read a dog's indication, and only time and intensive training together as a team can achieve that end.

CRIMINAL WORK

Most people, when they look at the characteristics of the ideal police dog would believe at first glance that there is some trait missing. Where is the word 'aggression'? Surely all general-purpose police dogs are 'nasty'?

This could not be further from the truth. A dog who is naturally nasty and aggressive is a liability on the streets. What we want to achieve is controlled aggression which we can turn on and off like a tap.

Teaching a dog to bite is an extension of the dog's play instinct. Most of us, at one time or another, have played 'tug of war' with our pet dog, usually with their favourite toy. The bite is taught in a similar fashion, whereby the toy is a piece of hessian sacking, and the dog is encouraged to play tug of war with it. This is called 'ragging' the dog. The dog is always allowed to win, and very soon becomes confident and possessive with the rag. Gradually, the hessian is wound around the trainer's arm, and the dog is encouraged to play with the rag on the arm in exactly the same way as before. There is no intent by the dog to hurt the trainer, and no aggression, but they can be hard at times!

As the dog becomes more confident, an element of discipline is brought in so that the trainer can control just when he wants the dog to release the rag.

You may say that you have seen police dogs be aggressive towards crowds, and this is true. Any dog worth his salt will be protective towards his handler, an instinct that many a handler has been glad of when faced by hostile crowds. However, the dog is always kept on a short lead to control that aggression, and the dog should never be over-encouraged in the exercise. After all, the law states that any person can use "as much force as is necessary" to defend himself, and anything more constitutes an assault.

INSTINCT

So, in conclusion, what instincts are used to train police dogs?
- Retrieve Instinct: tracking, searching for persons or property.
- Hunting Instinct: tracking and searching.
- Play Instinct: tracking, searching and biting.
- Protective Instinct: use of controlled aggression.

The protective instinct is used in this display of controlled aggression.
Photo courtesy: The Metropolitan Police.

CHAPTER ELEVEN

GUN DOGS

As the name suggests, the modern gun dog has been developed through selective breeding for the purpose of assisting the sporting hunter in the pursuit of game. Without considering individual breeds, gun dogs can conveniently be grouped into four categories that indicate the broad scope of their duties in the shooting field: retrievers; hunting and flushing dogs (spaniels); pointers and setters; and the hunt, point and retrieve breeds (HPRs).

GUN DOG INSTINCTS   By Tenant Brownlee

In one sense, gun dogs are no different from any other breed, in that all domesticated dogs have certain attributes in common that can be traced back to their wild ancestors. For example, they operate best when in a pack, and are very conscious of their status within that pack. They are quick to associate stimuli with actions, sometimes to the extent that a conditioned reflex establishes itself, and they will take any opportunity to elevate their status within the pack. Gun dogs bred for work (as opposed to those primarily show bred, where there may have been some genetic 'degeneration' of the working drive) exhibit a highly specialised set of behaviours, which may be regarded as survival-driven

Photo: Carol Ann Johnson.

One aspect of gundog training consists of encouraging certain inbuilt drives and modifying others.

Photo: Graham Cox.

or instinctive. Through their genes, these behaviour patterns or drives are already programmed into the gun dog's mind at birth, and will have a profound effect on his actions and behaviour throughout his life.

These patterns can be considered together as a form of 'predatory aggression' or as a set of compulsions – to scent, hunt, flush, chase, catch, kill and carry game. Every gun dog possesses all these drives, to a greater or lesser degree, and any consideration of the gun dog's mind must take them fully into account. In the wild, these are the behaviours that would enable a dog to survive, and successful performance results in a reward for the dog – his food. Food obviously constitutes powerful positive reinforcement, and a gun dog will always tend to repeat the actions that procure it. This also means that any training the gun dog undergoes will always take second place in his mind to its inbred compulsions – a fact that any gun dog trainer will confirm.

Humans, having developed different gun dog breeds to suit their own shooting needs, find it convenient when training and working them to categorise and separate the several predatory gun dog drives to fit in with human thinking. This can sometimes lead to training problems, because we have to accept the dog for what it is (although selective breeding over the years can, to some extent, have an effect). We have to realise that gun dogs, since they do not think in human terms, do not make any distinction between what the human trainer might regard as being right or wrong. It is all one to them. A gun dog does not separate hunting from retrieving in its mind; neither is there an essential difference between flushing and catching its quarry. In fact, in the latter instance, one action often flows into the other and, in certain circumstances, is the prelude to killing. We ought not to be surprised at this, because it is no more than a hound, for example, does when it catches a fox. If a trained gun dog found itself thrown on to its own resources away from human influence (as it would do if it found itself living wild), that is how it would find its food.

TRAINING

We can look at gun dog training in two ways, each of which impinges on the way a gun dog's mind operates. One aspect consists of encouraging certain of the inbuilt drives and of modifying others. The other aspect consists of teaching the dog certain non-instinctive actions which will always remain subservient to his instinctive behaviour. Remaining seated in the face of temptation, as a retriever might be called upon to do in close proximity to a fluttering pheasant, is one example; learning to drop at the sound of a whistle command is another.

Fortunately, selective breeding has ensured that the desire to kill game has been suppressed, to some extent, and partially replaced with the desire to carry dead and wounded game to the leader of the pack – the trainer or the owner. Nevertheless, it is not uncommon for the desire to kill to resurface. I have watched a Springer, a soft, affectionate bitch that I knew to have a reliable mouth, lift a young rabbit from a tuft of grass and, presumably because she was in close proximity to other dogs, deliberately kill it. Catching unshot game, or 'pegging' in gun dog parlance, can lead to killing. It is not unknown for dogs who have been pecked or scratched by a wounded bird to exact the ultimate revenge. There are imponderables in this area of gun dog behaviour. Sometimes a hitherto soft-mouthed animal will start damaging dead and killing wounded game for no obvious reason, and more than one gun dog has been known to make off with a retrieve and make a meal of it.

The chasing drive is worth some consideration, being the prelude to catching game. I take the view that it lies at the core of gun dog behaviour. The command to retrieve is no more than an order to chase game; as far as the dog is concerned, it is a reward, and one that is never refused. When it gets the order to retrieve, a gun dog often has no idea whether or not the game – a pheasant, let us say – is dead or wounded. If it is wounded, the chances are strong that the dog will have to chase it in order to gather his retrieve, and, from his point of view, will have been told to chase. Yet, throughout his training, he will have been conditioned not to chase game. It can be a delicate balance.

The situation with the hunting spaniel is even more interesting. Frequently, the dog will find and flush ground game in heavy cover, from where he has to move the game into the open. This involves chasing by sight for a short distance. As soon as the quarry breaks cover, the dog is then expected to drop without command and watch the game run away while its handler raises his gun to it. Should the rabbit be shot but not killed, the dog is expected to chase it once more, this time in order to retrieve it. Here is a situation ripe for causing confusion in the dog's mind, and it is to the credit of both gun dog and trainer that a fully-trained and experienced Spaniel will learn to cope with this situation. In effect, the dog is being asked to turn instinct on, then off and then on again. The weak link in this particular chain, of course, is ensuring that, as the game breaks into the open or flushes, the dog stops. This, in turn, involves reinforcing a non-instinctive action into the animal's genetically motivated behaviour pattern during its training. In passing, it may be mentioned that it is a rock upon which many a Spaniel-training enterprise has foundered.

The urge to point game is present in all breeds of gun dog, but far more so in Pointers, Setters and HPRs than in Spaniels and Retrievers. Just as Retriever puppies of only a few weeks can be seen to pick up and carry small objects, so Pointer puppies will often be found pointing things that excite their curiosity. Nevertheless, Retrievers and Spaniels will sometimes be observed pointing game before flushing it, and some trainers encourage this. Others discourage it, particularly in the case of spaniels, because they prefer the dog to go straight into the flush with no hesitation. The sensitivity of a gun dog's olfactory system is well-known, and, of course, pointing is a result of this and it is not in the least unusual for a dog to indicate game thirty or so yards away, if the wind and scenting conditions are right.

NON-INSTINCTIVE SKILLS

There is no real mystery about how a gun dog trainer approaches the business of schooling his pupils in sitting, dropping at a distance, responding to the recall and other skills of a non-instinctive nature. Collectively, they might fall under the heading of obedience, although perhaps of a less rigid kind than conventional competition-based 'obedience' training. To reach his full potential in the shooting field, a gun dog is expected to use a degree of initiative, because he is quite likely to be working out of sight of his handler for much of the time. A Retriever might well have to follow (take a line) on a wounded bird that brings him into the close proximity of many unshot birds without deviating from his original quarry. There has been some speculation about how a dog does this, and it has been postulated that it is following a 'blood' scent. However, many wounded pheasants do not leave a physical trail of blood, so there would seem to be some other explanation. A 'shocked' scent has been suggested. A spaniel hunting for game has to learn to discriminate between the scent drifts that come to him on the wind and identify which are worth following up. A canine automaton would be of little use in such circumstances. Frequently, gun dogs will apparently disobey their handler's direction signals simply because their nose tells them where a retrieve lies.

Like any other dog trainer, the gun dog trainer makes use of Pavlovian

Gun dogs often work out of sight of their handler, and must use some degree of initiative while remaining under control.

Photo: Steve Nash.

The retrieve instinct is strong enough to keep the gundog working, despite the obstacles he encounters.

Photos: Steve Nash

The game is brought back to the handler with the minimum of mouthing.

Photo: Steve Nash.

theory when bedding-in non-instinctive skills along with positive reinforcement and reward. Some begin this process early in a puppy's life, and many gun dogs are pretty well-behaved animals before more serious field training gets under way. There is logic in this, since it is counter-productive to try to modify any instinctive drives if the young gun dog does not look to his trainer as the number one being in his life. If a dog will not, for example, approach his trainer happily when he is called with nothing in his mouth, there is no point in trying to refine his retrieving abilities. Nor is it feasible to move on to teaching a gun dog to respond to direction signals if the trainer cannot make the dog drop at a distance by voice or whistle. There is a further and perhaps less obvious reason for giving any gun dog a thorough elementary course of 'obedience'. The dog becomes more focused on the trainer, and, while he will never 'forget' his natural instincts, he tends to be less self-centred in the presence of game.

So, the aim is to reach a happy medium once a dog has been trained so that he will respond willingly to commands, and yet retain a degree of atavism (while still keeping an eye and an ear open for his handler) when actually working on game. If nothing else, this needs an alert canine mind, and a dog who is keen to please his owner.

Provided that they have been well-socialised as puppies, most modern gun dogs are very trainable. They are affectionate, they bond well with humans, and they usually have a submissive nature, although there are alpha dogs around with a streak of dominance that can be pretty challenging to deal with. Training them can involve a battle of wills, and it is interesting to note that this can apply to bitches as well as dogs – the general belief that bitches are 'easier' than dogs is not necessarily true. There is a phrase in a poem I once read concerning the folly of 'giving your heart to a dog to tear' that encapsulates the sense of anthropomorphism that gun dogs – or indeed any kind of dog – engender in some people. It must never be forgotten that, at bottom, gun dogs are animals with no sense of human value. Although they are sentient creatures, their needs deserving of our consideration, they do not feel guilt or experience remorse. They do not set out deliberately to annoy us – although with certain Cocker Spaniels I wonder just a little about this! Unfortunately, humans cannot say 'sorry' to a gun dog; but then, the reverse also applies.

THE HANDLER

We cannot reasonably consider the gun dog's mind without also giving a little thought to the mind of his handler, since they are intimately bound up with each another. There can be few people involved with gun dogs who have not, at one time or another, taken pleasure from physical contact with one; some, although they might not happily admit it in public, even indulge in petting and nonsense talk. This seems only right and proper, but, at the same time, there is a danger of attributing human emotion to the dog to the extent that the relationship can become one-sided while the dog tries to work its way up the status ladder. How, we might ask, remembering the parameters of the canine mind, is a gun dog expected to know that, while he might be allowed to take liberties in the domestic environment and do more or less as he pleases, he must change his attitude as soon as he starts work, and take second place to his handler's wishes? It is well-recognised that there are psychological factors at play in dog ownership, and this applies as much with gun dogs as with any other area of dog owning. The point was made earlier that it is the specialised development of certain predatory canine instincts that make the gun dog mind what it is. Any owner who ignores that basic truth does so entirely at their own risk.

CHAPTER TWELVE

SUMMING UP

In his book *The Evolution of Canine Social Behaviour*, Dr Roger Abrantes talks about "my crusade to clean up the mess of terms in the behaviour sciences". He also says that "there is a great confusion, not only in popular literature, but among scholars, over the definitions of some concepts used to explain behaviour."

When meeting and talking to owners of family dogs – pet owners, if you like – we have come to the conclusion that Dr Abrantes is quite right. Owning a dog used to be just another facet of family life. Of course, there were problems, but these were sorted at home by the family – usually the mother! People then, in both town and country, were nearer to nature than they are today.

Now, dog owners watch numerous television programmes on dog training and behaviour. Not all the presenters have the same advice to give; it varies considerably, as do the scientific terms they use. Then there are books, training manuals, training classes and behaviour counsellors, all offering conflicting advice with a bewildering array of terminology. No wonder people become worried about their dog's

It is your responsibility to give your dog a happy and fulfilling life.

behaviour. Quite often, so-called problem behaviour is behaviour which, to the dog, is normal, but which is completely misunderstood by the owner.

In this book we have tried to explain in simple terms why a dog behaves as he does. We hope that some of the anecdotes about our own dogs will make this clearer. Once you begin to understand your dog and why he reacts the way that he does in certain situations, you should find it much easier to train him – and trained he must be. There is much anti-dog feeling in the Western world today, made worse by badly-behaved dogs. We have covered basic, but essential, obedience. Once your dog has learned that, you can take him on to 'higher education', depending on his capabilities.

As in other animals, including humans, no dog is perfect. It is said that we like our friends because we know and accept their faults. The same is true with our dogs. Maybe you hoped that your bright, bouncy puppy would grow up to be an Obedience Champion, only to find that he is much happier playing with the children. But then, you may have had a secret hope that your son would become a famous surgeon, and he has ended up being very happy tinkering with cars! In both cases, you will, no doubt, love them both just the same.

Today, we seldom allow our dogs to carry out the roles for which they have been programmed. Man's unemployment problem is self-inflicted. Unfortunately, he has also brought about unemployment in the dog world. Unemployed dogs are usually unhappy and get into trouble. The psychologist Mihaly Csiksnentmihalyi has carried out a great deal of research into happiness in humans. He came to the conclusion that using too few skills generates boredom and anxiety, which may be the biggest threats to human happiness. The same might well apply to dogs who are denied an outlet for their undoubted qualities.

The last three chapters have taken us 'behind the scenes' in the selection and training of assistance dogs, working dogs and gun dogs. Many of these (although not guide dogs, who are purpose-bred) come from Welfare organisations or have been passed on from family homes because of various problems. Most probably, they got into trouble because they were under-exercised, bored and frustrated. Although there are always some dogs who will be better suited to a working life rather than family life, many others would have settled happily as family pets, if only their owner had been able to understand them.

Always keep in mind the purpose for which your dog was originally bred: gun dogs, for work with the gun; scent hounds, for hunting; sight hounds, for coursing; guard dogs, for police work; terriers, for catching rabbits; and so on. For those who want them, there are innumerable canine sports which cater for specialist breeds, where a dog can use the instincts of his own particular breed: Field Trials and scurries for gun dogs; Sheepdog Trials for Border Collies; Terrier Racing; Sled Dog Racing; Carting for Bernese and similar breeds; Police Dog Trials, Greyhound and Afghan Racing and Lure Racing, to name but a few. Whatever breed your dog, there will be something which can provide an outlet for his instinct and initiatives.

If you and your family dog have no ambition to take part in these specialised sports, there are other more general ones, which give the dog a chance to use his mind as well as his body, including Agility, Scent Hurdling, Frisbee-catching and more. Agility has become increasingly popular for family pets. There are smaller courses for small dogs, and slower courses for veterans. Dogs, owners and spectators all enjoy this sport.

However, if you are not competitive-minded, there is plenty that you can do together to make life interesting. Most dogs, especially gun dogs, enjoy swimming and retrieving. Take your dog down to the sea or by a river, and let him have fun retrieving from the water. Most dogs can be taught to retrieve – some more enthusiastically than others – but once a dog has been taught, it opens up endless opportunities. He can fetch the newspaper, your slippers, the post, his lead. It is not difficult to teach him to fetch things by name, and it always impresses visitors! Make sure he has plenty of fun – it is good for both of you. When out for a walk in the country, play with your dog and have him jump fallen trees, ditches, low walls – anything he is capable of jumping. Teach him to track back and find something you have dropped, such as a glove. This exercise can be very useful if you have lost something for real. Hide things in long grass or heather. Fuzzy, our Chihuahua, derives endless pleasure from searching for a fir cone we have handled. She never gives up, and, however long it takes, always comes back with the right one. If several people are out together, let someone lay a track or go and hide, and have the dog find them.

So-called Toy dogs have the same need for physical and mental exercise as larger dogs. They do have the advantage that, if their owner is not capable of walking long distances, the dog can still get a lot of exercise playing ball in the garden.

No-one forced you to have a dog – you chose to do so. We have taken away from the dog his right to fend for himself, and brought him in to join our human pack. So it is our responsibility to look after our dogs and to supply their needs – feed them, exercise them and train them. Dogs are usually intelligent animals, but man is supposedly the most intelligent creature on earth, even if there are times when this seems doubtful! Surely it is not too much to ask for us to understand our dogs? They try very hard to understand us, and that cannot be very easy.

In recent times, man's attitude to dogs has changed considerably, even if the dog has changed very little. This makes it even more important to have a well-behaved dog than it was several years ago. Like a well-behaved child, a well-behaved dog can enjoy life much more than a badly-behaved one. He can be taken on outings or visiting friends and mix with other dogs and people, because you can rely on his behaviour. There is much anti-dog feeling in the Western world, and untrained dogs only add to the problem.

Do not forget to have fun with your dog. Take a look around you when you are walking your dog in the park or on the beach; you will find that the happiest and most friendly people are those with dogs.